Francis James Child

Poems of Religious Sorrow, Comfort, Counsel and Aspiration

Francis James Child

Poems of Religious Sorrow, Comfort, Counsel and Aspiration

ISBN/EAN: 9783337182427

Printed in Europe, USA, Canada, Australia, Japan

Cover: Foto ©Lupo / pixelio.de

More available books at **www.hansebooks.com**

POEMS OF RELIGIOUS SORROW, COMFORT, COUNSEL, AND ASPIRATION

SELECTED BY F. J. CHILD

'T IS LIFE WHEREOF OUR NERVES ARE SCANT,
OH LIFE, NOT DEATH, FOR WHICH WE PANT;
MORE LIFE, AND FULLER, THAT I WANT.

———◆———

I AM COME THAT THEY MIGHT HAVE LIFE, AND THAT
THEY MIGHT HAVE IT MORE ABUNDANTLY

NEW YORK
PUBLISHED BY HURD AND HOUGHTON
BOSTON: E. P. DUTTON AND COMPANY
1866

PRAY for the health of all that are diseasèd,
  Confession unto all that are convicted,
And patience unto all that are displeasèd,
  And comfort unto all that are afflicted,
And mercy unto all that have offended,
And grace to all, that all may be amended!

THIS little volume contains about thirty more pieces than one published with the same title three years ago. The additions are mainly from the Rev. T. V. Fosbery's "Hymns and Poems for the Sick and Suffering,"— an excellent collection, which may suit the case of many pious and trustful persons better than this.

It is necessary to say that the titles given to some of the pieces are not those of the authors, and that, having a practical object in view, I have often taken only so much of a poem as answered my purpose. But in no instance have the words of an author been altered, though there are phrases here and there which I do not approve.

All the poems by American authors, excepting one anonymous piece, are here printed with the express permission of the lawful proprietors. Thanks are especially due to Messrs. Ticknor and Fields for their liberality in this respect.

F. J. C.

CHRISTMAS, 1865.

For one whose life lay bound, long years,
In cold obstruction thrilled with fears,
Whose daily bread was salt with tears:

Whom the all-pleasant light of day
Woke to a scarce-forgot dismay,
Whose misery sleep might not allay:

Whose soul seemed, by an awful lot,
Fixed in a void but ghastly spot,
Where hope came not, where God was not:

Yet now, through grace, essays to trust
God is, is merciful as just,
And souls outlive all pangs of dust.

For friends, ah, many friends! who find
From ills of body, heart, or mind
No ease, except to be resigned:

Who, in the countless paths of pain,
Weeping, sow seeds of precious grain, —
One day to bring back sheaves again!

For all, who, battling through this life
In anguish steeped, with evil rife,
Faint with the unremitting strife:

Dear, for the sorrows they endure,
And dear to pitying God most sure,
Who makes his own by all means pure.

POEMS OF SORROW AND COMFORT.

EVIL.

Evil, every living hour,
  Holds us in its wilful hand,
Savé as Thou, essential Power,
  Mayst be gracious to withstand:
Pain within the subtle flesh,
  Heavy lids that cannot close,
Hearts that hope will not refresh, —
  Hand of Healing! interpose.

Tyranny's strong breath is tainting
  Nature's sweet and vivid air;
Nations silently are fainting,
  Or upgather in despair:
Not to those distracted wills
  Trust the judgment of their woes;
While the cup of anguish fills,
  Arm of Justice! interpose.

Evil.

Pleasures night and day are hovering
   Round their prey of weary hours,
Weakness and unrest discovering
   In the best of human powers:
Ere the fond delusions tire,
   Ere envenomed passion grows
From the root of vain desire,—
   Mind of Wisdom! interpose.

Now no more in tuneful motion
   Life with love and duty glides;
Reason's meteor-lighted ocean
   Bears us down its mazy tides;
Head is clear and hand is strong,
   But our heart no haven knows;
Sun of Truth! the night is long,—
   Let Thy radiance interpose!

THE TWO VOICES.

A STILL small voice spake unto me:
" Thou art so full of misery,
Were it not better not to be?"

Then to the still small voice I said,
" Let me not cast in endless shade
What is so wonderfully made."

To which the voice did urge reply:
" To-day I saw the dragon-fly
Come from the wells where he did lie.

" An inner impulse rent the veil
Of his old husk: from head to tail
Came out clear plates of sapphire mail.

" He dried his wings: like gauze they grew:
Through crofts and pastures wet with dew
A living flash of light he flew."

I said, "When first the world began,
Young Nature through five cycles ran,
And in the sixth she moulded man.

"She gave him mind, the lordliest
Proportion, and, above the rest,
Dominion in the head and breast."

Thereto the silent voice replied,
"Self-blinded are you by your pride:
Look up through night: the world is wide.

"This truth within thy mind rehearse,
That in a boundless universe
Is boundless better, boundless worse.

"Think you this mould of hopes and fears
Could find no statelier than his peers
In yonder hundred million spheres?"

It spake, moreover, in my mind:
"Though thou wert scattered to the wind,
Yet is there plenty of the kind."

Then did my response clearer fall:
"No compound of this earthly ball
Is like another, all in all."

The Two Voices.

To which he answered scoffingly,
" Good soul! suppose I grant it thee,
Who'll weep for thy deficiency?

" Or will one beam be less intense,
When thy peculiar difference
Is cancelled in the world of sense?"

I would have said, " Thou canst not know,"
But my full heart, that worked below,
Rained through my sight its overflow.

Again the voice spake unto me:
" Thou art so steeped in misery,
Surely 't were better not to be.

" Thine anguish will not let thee sleep,
Nor any train of reason keep:
Thou canst not think, but thou wilt weep."

I said, " The years with change advance:
If I make dark my countenance,
I shut my life from happier chance.

" Some turn this sickness yet might take,
Even yet." But he : " What drug can make
A withered palsy cease to shake?"

I wept, "Though I should die, I know
That all about the thorn will blow
In tufts of rosy-tinted snow;

"And men, through novel spheres of thought
Still moving after truth long sought,
Will learn new things when I am not."

"Yet," said the secret voice, "some time,
Sooner or later, will gray prime
Make thy grass hoar with early rime.

"Not less swift souls that yearn for light,
Rapt after heaven's starry flight,
Would sweep the tracts of day and night.

"Not less the bee would range her cells,
The furzy prickle fire the dells,
The foxglove cluster dappled bells."

I said that "all the years invent;
Each month is various to present
The world with some development.

"Were this not well, to bide mine hour,
Though watching from a ruined tower
How grows the day of human power?"

The Two Voices.

"The highest-mounted mind," he said,
"Still sees the sacred morning spread
The silent summit overhead.

"Will thirty seasons render plain
Those lonely lights that still remain,
Just breaking over land and main?

"Or make that morn, from his cold crown
And crystal silence creeping down,
Flood with full daylight glebe and town?

"Forerun thy peers, thy time, and let
Thy feet, millenniums hence, be set
In midst of knowledge dreamed not yet:

"Thou hast not gained a real height,
Nor art thou nearer to the light,
Because the scale is infinite.

"'T were better not to breathe or speak
Than cry for strength, remaining weak,
And seem to find, but still to seek.

"Moreover, but to seem to find
Asks what thou lackest, thought resigned,
A healthy frame, a quiet mind."

I said, "When I am gone away,
'He dared not tarry,' men will say,
Doing dishonor to my clay."

"This is more vile," he made reply,
"To breathe and loathe, to live and sigh,
Than once from dread of pain to die.

"Sick art thou, — a divided will
Still heaping on the fear of ill
The fear of men, a coward still.

"Do men love thee? Art thou so bound
To men, that how thy name may sound
Will vex thee lying under ground?

"The memory of the withered leaf
In endless time is scarce more brief
Than of the garnered autumn-sheaf.

"Go, vexèd spirit, sleep in trust;
The right ear, that is filled with dust,
Hears little of the false or just."

"Hard task, to pluck resolve," I cried,
"From emptiness and the waste wide
Of that abyss, or scornful pride!

The Two Voices.

"Nay, — rather yet that I could raise
One hope that warmed me in the days
While still I yearned for human praise.

" When, wide in soul and bold of tongue,
Among the tents I paused and sung,
The distant battle flashed and rung.

" I sung the joyful pæan clear,
And, sitting, burnished without fear
The brand, the buckler, and the spear, —

" Waiting to strive a happy strife,
To war with falsehood to the knife,
And not to lose the good of life, —

" Some hidden principle to move,
To put together, part and prove,
And mete the bounds of hate and love, —

" As far as might be, to carve out
Free space for every human doubt,
That the whole mind might orb about, —

" To search through all I felt and saw,
The springs of life, the depths of awe,
And reach the law within the law:

"At least, not rotting like a weed,
But having sown some generous seed,
Fruitful of further thought and deed,

"To pass, when Life her light withdraws,
Not void of righteous self-applause,
Nor in a merely selfish cause, —

"In some good cause, not in mine own,
To perish, wept for, honored, known,
And like a warrior overthrown;

"Whose eyes are dim with glorious tears,
When, soiled with noble dust, he hears
His country's war-song thrill his ears:

"Then dying of a mortal stroke,
What time the foeman's line is broke,
And all the war is rolled in smoke."

"Yea!" said the voice, "thy dream was good,
While thou abodest in the bud:
It was the stirring of the blood.

"If Nature put not forth her power
About the opening of the flower,
Who is it that could live an hour?

"Then comes the check, the change, the fall:
Pain rises up, old pleasures pall:
There is one remedy for all.

"Yet hadst thou, through enduring pain,
Linked month to month with such a chain
Of knitted purport, all were vain.

"Thou hadst not between death and birth
Dissolved the riddle of the earth:
So were thy labor little worth.

"That men with knowledge merely played
I told thee, — hardly nigher made,
Though scaling slow from grade to grade;

"Much less this dreamer, deaf and blind,
Named man, may hope some truth to find
That bears relation to the mind.

"For every worm beneath the moon
Draws different threads, and late and soon
Spins, toiling out his own cocoon.

"Cry, faint not: — either Truth is born
Beyond the polar gleam forlorn,
Or in the gateways of the morn.

" Cry, faint not, climb : — the summits slope
Beyond the furthest flights of hope.
Wrapt in dense cloud from base to cope.

" Sometimes a little corner shines,
As over rainy mist inclines
A gleaming crag with belts of pines.

" I will go forward, sayest thou,
I shall not fail to find her now.
Look up, the fold is on her brow.

" If straight thy track, or if oblique,
Thou know'st not. Shadows thou dost strike,
Embracing cloud, Ixion-like ;

" And owning but a little more
Than beasts, abidest lame and poor,
Calling thyself a little lower

" Than angels. Cease to wail and brawl !
Why inch by inch to darkness crawl ?
There is one remedy for all."

" O dull, one-sided voice," said I,
" Wilt thou make everything a lie,
To flatter me that I may die ?

"I know that age to age succeeds,
Blowing a noise of tongues and deeds,
A dust of systems and of creeds.

"I cannot hide that some have striven,
Achieving calm, to whom was given
The joy that mixes man with Heaven:

"Who, rowing hard against the stream,
Saw distant gates of Eden gleam,
And did not dream it was a dream;

"But heard, by secret transport led,
Even in the charnels of the dead,
The murmur of the fountain-head, —

"Which did accomplish their desire,
Bore and forbore, and did not tire,
Like Stephen, an unquenchèd fire.

"He heeded not reviling tones,
Nor sold his heart to idle moans,
Though cursed and scorned, and bruised with
    stones:

"But looking upward, full of grace,
He prayed, and from a happy place
God's glory smote him on the face."

The sullen answer slid betwixt:
" Not that the grounds of hope were fixed,
The elements were kindlier mixed."

I said, " I toil beneath the curse,
But, knowing not the universe,
I fear to slide from bad to worse :

" And that, in seeking to undo
One riddle, and to find the true,
I knit a hundred others new :

" Or that this anguish fleeting hence,
Unmanacled from bonds of sense,
Be fixed and frozen to permanence :

" For I go, weak from suffering here;
Naked I go, and void of cheer :
What is it that I may not fear ? "

" Consider well," the voice replied,
" His face that two hours since hath died;
Wilt thou find passion, pain, or pride ?

" Will he obey when one commands ?
Or answer should one press his hands ?
He answers not, nor understands.

The Two Voices.

"His palms are folded on his breast:
There is no other thing expressed
But long disquiet merged in rest.

"His lips are very mild and meek:
Though one should smite him on the cheek,
And on the mouth, he will not speak.

"His little daughter, whose sweet face
He kissed, taking his last embrace,
Becomes dishonor to her race, —

"His sons grow up that bear his name,
Some grow to honor, some to shame, —
But he is chill to praise or blame.

"He will not hear the north-wind rave,
Nor, moaning, household shelter crave
From winter rains that beat his grave.

"High up the vapors fold and swim:
About him broods the twilight dim:
The place he knew forgetteth him."

"If all be dark, vague voice," I said.
"These things are wrapt in doubt and dread,
Nor canst thou show the dead are dead.

"The sap dries up: the plant declines:
A deeper tale my heart divines:
Know I not Death? the outward signs?

"I found him when my years were few:
A shadow on the graves I knew,
And darkness in the village yew.

"From grave to grave the shadow crept:
In her still place the morning wept:
Touched by his feet the daisy slept.

"The simple senses crowned his head:
'Omega! thou art Lord,' they said,
'We find no motion in the dead.'

"Why, if man rot in dreamless ease,
Should that plain fact, as taught by these,
Not make him sure that he shall cease?

"Who forged that other influence,
That heat of inward evidence,
By which he doubts against the sense?

"He owns the fatal gift of eyes
That read his spirit blindly wise,
Not simple as a thing that dies.

The Two Voices.

"Here sits he shaping wings to fly;
His heart forebodes a mystery:
He names the name Eternity.

"That type of Perfect in his mind
In Nature can he nowhere find.
He sows himself on every wind.

"He seems to hear a Heavenly Friend,
And through thick veils to apprehend
A labor working to an end.

"The end and the beginning vex
His reason: many things perplex,
With motions, checks, and counter-checks.

"He knows a baseness in his blood
At such strange war with something good,
He may not do the thing he would.

"Heaven opens inward, chasms yawn,
Vast images in glimmering dawn,
Half shown, are broken and withdrawn.

"Ah! sure within him and without,
Could his dark wisdom find it out,
There must be answer to his doubt.

"But thou canst answer not again:
With thine own weapon art thou slain,
Or thou wilt answer but in vain.

"The doubt would rest, I dare not solve:
In the same circle we revolve:
Assurance only breeds resolve."

As when a billow, blown against,
Falls back, the voice with which I fenced
A little ceased, but recommenced:

"Where wert thou when thy father played
In his free field, and pastime made,
A merry boy in sun and shade?

"A merry boy they called him then.
He sat upon the knees of men
In days that never come again.

"Before the little ducts began
To feed thy bones with lime, and ran
Their course, till thou wert also man:

"Who took a wife, who reared his race,
Whose wrinkles gathered on his face,
Whose troubles number with his days:

"A life of nothings, nothing worth,
From that first nothing ere his birth
To that last nothing under earth!"

"These words," I said, "are like the rest,
No certain clearness, but at best
A vague suspicion of the breast:

"But if I grant, thou might'st defend
The thesis which thy words intend,—
That to begin implies to end;

"Yet how should I for certain hold,
Because my memory is so cold,
That I first was in human mould?

"I cannot make this matter plain,
But I would shoot, howe'er in vain,
A random arrow from the brain.

"It may be that no life is found,
Which only to one engine bound
Falls off, but cycles always round.

"As old mythologies relate,
Some draught of Lethe might await
The slipping through from state to state.

"As here we find in trances, men
Forget the dream that happens then,
Until they fall in trance again.

"So might we, if our state were such
As one before, remember much,
For those two likes might meet and touch.

"But, if I lapsed from nobler place,
Some legend of a fallen race
Alone might hint of my disgrace;

"Some vague emotion of delight
In gazing up an Alpine height,
Some yearning toward the lamps of night.

"Or if through lower lives I came —
Though all experience past became
Consolidate in mind and frame —

"I might forget my weaker lot;
For is not our first year forgot?
The haunts of memory echo not.

"And men, whose reason long was blind,
From cells of madness unconfined,
Oft lose whole years of darker mind.

The Two Voices.   25

"Much more, if first I floated free,
As naked essence, must I be
Incompetent of memory:

"For memory dealing but with time,
And he with matter, could she climb
Beyond her own material prime?

"Moreover, something is or seems,
That touches me with mystic gleams,
Like glimpses of forgotten dreams —

"Of something felt, like something here;
Of something done, I know not where;
Such as no language may declare."

The still voice laughed. "I talk," said he,
"Not with thy dreams. Suffice it thee
Thy pain is a reality."

"But thou," said I, "hast missed thy mark,
Who sought'st to wreck my mortal ark,
By making all the horizon dark.

"Why not set forth, if I should do
This rashness, that which might ensue
With this old soul in organs new?

"Whatever crazy sorrow saith,
No life that breathes with human breath
Has ever truly longed for death.

" 'T is life, whereof our nerves are scant,
Oh life, not death, for which we pant;
More life, and fuller, that I want."

I ceased, and sat as one forlorn.
Then said the voice, in quiet scorn,
" Behold, it is the Sabbath morn."

And I arose, and I released
The casement, and the light increased
With freshness in the dawning east.

Like softened airs that blowing steal,
When meres begin to uncongeal,
The sweet church-bells began to peal.

On to God's house the people prest:
Passing the place where each must rest,
Each entered like a welcome guest.

One walked between his wife and child,
With measured footfall firm and mild,
And now and then he gravely smiled.

The Two Voices.

The prudent partner of his blood
Leaned on him, faithful, gentle, good,
Wearing the rose of womanhood.

And in their double love secure,
The little maiden walked demure,
Pacing with downward eyelids pure.

These three made unity so sweet,
My frozen heart began to beat,
Remembering its ancient heat.

I blest them, and they wandered on:
I spoke, but answer came there none:
The dull and bitter voice was gone.

A second voice was at mine ear,
A little whisper silver-clear,
A murmur, "Be of better cheer."

As from some blissful neighborhood,
A notice faintly understood,
"I see the end, and know the good."

A little hint to solace woe,
A hint, a whisper breathing low,
"I may not speak of what I know."

Like an Æolian harp, that wakes
No certain air, but overtakes
Far thought with music that it makes, —

Such seemed the whisper at my side:
"What is 't thou know'st, sweet voice?" I cried.
"A hidden hope," the voice replied:

So heavenly-toned, that in that hour
From out my sullen heart a power
Broke, like the rainbow from the shower,

To feel, although no tongue can prove,
That every cloud that spreads above,
And veileth love, itself is love.

And forth into the fields I went,
And Nature's living motion lent
The pulse of hope to discontent.

I wondered at the bounteous hours,
The slow result of winter showers:
You scarce could see the grass for flowers.

I wondered, while I paced along:
The woods were filled so full with song,
There seemed no room for sense of wrong.

So variously seemed all things wrought,
I marvelled how the mind was brought
To anchor by one gloomy thought;

And wherefore rather I made choice
To commune with that barren voice,
Than him that said, "Rejoice! rejoice!"

LIFE SHALL LIVE FOR EVERMORE.

My own dim life should teach me this,
    That life shall live for evermore, —
    Else earth is darkness at the core,
And dust and ashes all that is:

This round of green, this orb of flame,
    Fantastic beauty; such as lurks
    In some wild Poet, when he works
Without a conscience or an aim.

What then were God to such as I?
    'T were hardly worth my while to choose
    Of things all mortal, or to use
A little patience ere I die.

'T were best at once to sink to peace;
    Like birds the charming serpent draws,
    To drop head-foremost in the jaws
Of vacant darkness, and to cease.

Yet if some voice that man could trust
    Should murmur from the narrow house,
    "The cheeks drop in; the body bows;
Man dies; nor is there hope in dust":

Might I not say, "Yet even here,
    But for one hour, O Love, I strive
    To keep so sweet a thing alive"?
But I should turn mine ears and hear

The moanings of the homeless sea,
    The sound of streams that, swift or slow,
    Draw down æonian hills, and sow
The dust of continents to be:

And Love would answer with a sigh,
    "The sound of that forgetful shore
    Will change my sweetness more and more,
Half dead to know that I shall die."

Oh me, what profits it to put
    An idle case! If Death were seen
    At first as Death, Love had not been,
Or been in narrowest working shut,

Mere fellowship of sluggish moods,
    Or, in his coarsest satyr-shape,
    Had bruised the herb and crushed the grape,
And basked and battened in the woods.

EVIL SHALL END IN GOOD.

Oh, yet we trust that somehow good
   Will be the final goal of ill,
   To pangs of nature, sins of will,
Defects of doubt, and taints of blood;

That nothing walks with aimless feet;
   That not one life shall be destroyed,
   Or cast as rubbish to the void,
When God hath made the pile complete;

That not a worm is cloven in vain;
   That not a moth with vain desire
   Is shrivelled in a fruitless fire,
Or but subserves another's gain.

Behold, we know not anything;
   I can but trust that good shall fall
   At last — far off — *at last*, to all,
And every winter change to spring.

So runs my dream: but what am I?
   An infant crying in the night:
   An infant crying for the light:
And with no language but a cry.

THE wish, that of the living whole
   No life may fail beyond the grave,
   Derives it not from what we have
The likest God within the soul?

Are God and Nature then at strife,
   That Nature lends such evil dreams?
   So careful of the type she seems,
So careless of the single life;

That I, considering everywhere
   Her secret meaning in her deeds,
   And finding that of fifty seeds
She often brings but one to bear,

I falter where I firmly trod,
   And falling with my weight of cares
   Upon the great world's altar-stairs,
That slope through darkness up to God,

I stretch lame hands of faith, and grope,
   And gather dust and chaff, and call

To what I feel is Lord of all,
And faintly trust the larger hope.

"So careful of the type?" but no:
From scarpèd cliff and quarried stone
She cries, "A thousand types are gone:
I care for nothing, all shall go.

"Thou makest thine appeal to me:
I bring to life, I bring to death:
The spirit does but mean the breath:
I know no more." And he, shall he,

Man, her last work, who seemed so fair,
Such splendid purpose in his eyes,
Who rolled the psalm to wintry skies,
Who built him fanes of fruitless prayer,

Who trusted God was love indeed,
And love Creation's final law —
Though Nature, red in tooth and claw
With ravine, shrieked against his creed —

Who loved, who suffered countless ills,
Who battled for the True, the Just,
Be blown about the desert dust,
Or sealed within the iron hills?

Evil shall end in Good.

No more? A monster then, a dream,
  A discord. Dragons of the prime,
  That tare each other in their slime,
Were mellow music matched with him.

Oh life as futile, then, as frail!
  Oh for thy voice to soothe and bless!
  What hope of answer, or redress?
BEHIND THE VEIL, BEHIND THE VEIL!

OPPOSITIONS OF SCIENCE.

I TRUST I have not wasted breath:
   I think we are not wholly brain,
   Magnetic mockeries; not in vain,
Like Paul with beasts, I fought with Death.

Not only cunning casts in clay:
   Let Science prove we are, and then
   What matters Science unto men?—
At least to me?—I would not stay.

THROUGH A GLASS DARKLY.

THE human spirits saw I on a day,
Sitting and looking each a different way;
And hardly tasking, subtly questioning,
Another spirit went around the ring
To each and each: and as he ceased his say,
Each after each, I heard them singly sing,
Some querulously high, some softly, sadly low,
We know not, — what avails to know?
We know not, — wherefore need we know?
This answer gave they still unto his suing, —
We know not, let us do as we are doing.

Dost thou not know that these things only seem?
I know not, let me dream my dream.
Are dust and ashes fit to make a treasure?
I know not, let me take my pleasure.
What shall avail the knowledge thou hast sought?
I know not, let me think my thought.
What is the end of strife?
I know not, let me live my life.

How many days or e'er thou mean'st to move?
I know not, let me love my love.
Were not things old once new?
I know not, let me do as others do.
And when the rest were overpast,
I know not, I will do my duty, said the last.

Thy duty do? rejoined the voice,
Ah do it, do it, and rejoice;
But shalt thou then, when all is done,
Enjoy a love, embrace a beauty
Like these, that may be seen and won
In life, whose course will then be run:
Or wilt thou be where there is none?
I know not, I will do my duty.

And taking up the word around, above, below,
Some querulously high, some softly, sadly low,
We know not, sang they all, nor ever need we
    know!
We know not, sang they, what avails to know?
Whereat the questioning spirit, some short space,
Though unabashed, stood quiet in his place.
But as the echoing chorus died away,
And to their dreams the rest returned apace,
By the one spirit I saw him kneeling low,
And in a silvery whisper heard him say:
Truly, thou knowst not, and thou needst not
    know;

Hope only, hope thou, and believe alway.
I also know not, and I need not know,
Only with questionings pass I to and fro,
Perplexing these that sleep, and in their folly
Imbreeding doubt and sceptic melancholy;
Till that their dreams deserting, they with me,
Come all to this true ignorance and thee.

Ich leb', und weiss nicht wie lang;
Ich sterb', und weiss nicht wann;
Ich fahr', und weiss nicht wohin;
Mich wundert dass ich fröhlich bin!

A WORLD WITHOUT GOD.

O'er throngs of men around I cast mine eyes,
While each to separate work his hand applies;
The mean who toil for food, the proud for fame,
And crowds, by custom led, with scarce an aim.

Here busy dwarfs gigantic shadows chase,
As if they thus could grow a giant race;
Unknowing what they are, they fain would be
Such empty dreams as in their sleep they see.

There lives like glittering bubbles mount the sky,
Contemning earth, from whence they rose on high,
A moment catch the stars' eternal rays,
And burst and vanish in the moon's clear gaze.

Or torn by passion, swoln with falsest pride,
Betrayed by doubt that mocks each surer guide
The rebel heart, in self-enthroned disdain,
Its lawless weakness boasts, and penal pain.

A World without God.

Alone it loves to bleed, and groan apart,
And scorn the crowd who stir the seething mart,
Who each will own, befooled by ease and pelf,
Nor earth nor heaven beyond his shrivelled self.

And yet, O God! within each darkened soul
Is life akin to thy creation's whole,
That needs but will to see, and straight would
  find
The world one frame for one pervading Mind.

In all things round one sacred Power would know,
From thee diffused through all thy works be-
  low;
In every breath of life would hear thy call,
And All discern in Each, and Thee in All.

A truth too vast for spirits lost in sloth,
By self-indulgence marred of nobler growth,
Who bear about, in impotence and shame,
Their human reason's visionary name.

Oh! grant the crowds of earth may read thy
  plan,
And strive to reach the hope designed for man;
Though now shorn, stunted, twisted, withered,
  spent,
We dare not dream how high thy love's intent.

A World without God.

O God! 't were more than life to mouldering dust,
The hour that kindled men to thoughtful trust;
That taught our hearts to seek thy righteous will,
And so with love thy wisdom's task fulfil.

Redeemed from fear, and washed from lustful blot,
By faith we then might rise above our lot;
And like thy chosen few, restored within,
By hearts as morning pure might conquer sin!

FOR FAITH AND REVERENCE.

STRONG Son of God, immortal Love,
 Whom we, that have not seen thy face,
 By faith, and faith alone, embrace,
Believing where we cannot prove!

Thou wilt not leave us in the dust;
 Thou madest man, he knows not why;
 He thinks he was not made to die;
And thou hast made him: thou art just.

Thou seemest human and divine,
 The highest, holiest manhood, thou:
 Our wills are ours, we know not how,—
Our wills are ours, to make them thine.

Our little systems have their day;
 They have their day and cease to be;
 They are but broken lights of thee,
And thou, O Lord, art more than they.

For Faith and Reverence.

We have but faith; we cannot know;
   For knowledge is of things we see;
   And yet we trust it comes from thee,
A beam in darkness — let it grow!

Let knowledge grow from more to more,
   But more of reverence in us dwell,
   That mind and soul, according well,
May make one music, as before:

But vaster. We are fools and slight;
   We mock thee when we do not fear;
   But help thy foolish ones to bear,
Help thy vain worlds to bear thy light!

—— *Reverence is the bond for man*
   With all of best his eyes discern;
Love teaches more than Doctrine can,
   And no pure Hope will vainly yearn.

But all from depths of mystery grows,
   Which hide from us the root of things;
And good beyond what Science knows
   To man his Faith's high reason brings.

CHRIST IN THE WORLD.

AMID the gay and noisy throng
 Around me fluttering, wheeling, shining,
My ears are filled with shout and song,
 But yet my soul is still repining,

Mid bounding joy, and passion's glow,
 Mid sportive bursts of mutual gladness,
Thin shades arise from far below,
 Where boils a secret gulf of madness.

A quivering cheek, a faltering glance,
 One throb, one sigh, the whole revealing;
In all the flashing, whirling dance,
 I see a world of shipwreck reeling.

And 't is the worst despair to know,
 By pangs within my bosom aching,
How deep in each the root of woe,
 How many a heart is slowly breaking.

But while my sad bewildered view
    The wide confusion vainly traces,
One look I see serenely true,
    Among the false and loveless faces.

Like yon blue sky, when first it shows
    The storm-tost ship how Heaven hath pity;
Or some pure mountain-breeze that blows
    Its healing o'er a plague-struck city.

A voice not loud, like wind or wave,
    A look made low by conscious greatness,
Where all is calm, and deep, and grave,
    With a full soul's mature sedateness.

By Him subdued to thought and peace,
    The crowd no more in tumult wander;
The sounds of surging riot cease,
    And hearts high swoln devoutly ponder.

By His mild glance and sober power
    Renewed to tranquil aspiration,
My soul escapes the reckless hour,
    And learns his spirit's pure elation.

PLATO AND CHRIST.

Methinks, O Sage, a nobler lore than thine
  More steadfast comfort gives and holier peace;
And I am fed by wisdom more divine
  Than e'er inspired melodious tongues of Greece.

On other shores, beneath more eastern skies,
  Thy faith was once proclaimed from age to age,
Not sealed, a treasure for the proudly wise,
  But spread, a people's common heritage.

In saint and prophet burnt with keener flame
  Than e'er illumed thy gracious soul's delight;
In children's words, in songs of ancient fame
  Was known, ennobled many a festal rite.

And all that Athens breathed of high and true,
  With soaring thought and finely moulded speech,

In our dear Lord to act and being grew,
    Whose life was more than words could ever teach.

A heart that beat for every human woe,
    A choice in holiest purpose pure and strong,
A truth, sole morning-light of all below,
    A love triumphant over deadliest wrong.

In Him, thy God, O Plato, dwelt on earth,
    An open presence, clear of earthly ill;
The life which drew from him its heavenly birth
    In all who seek renews his perfect will.

So have we sufferings, so a trust like his,
    So large repentance, born with many a throe,
So zeal untired to better all that is,
    And peace of spirit even here below.

Then be it mine the cross with him to bear,
    And leave the flowery shades of Academe;
With him go mourning through the infected air
    Of grief and sin, and drink his bitter stream.

So clearness, meekness, and unfaltering might,
    Ungained, though bravely sought, O Sage, by thee,
Shall be my starry chaplet in the night,
    And in the coming dawn my crown shall be.

ON A LIFE MISSPENT IN VANITY AND PASSION.

I' vo piangendo i miei passati tempi,
   I quai posi in amar cosa mortale,
   Senza levarmi a volo, avend' io l' ale
Per dar forse di me non bassi esempi.

Tu, che vedi i miei mali indegni ed empi,
   Rè del cielo, invisibile, immortale,
   Soccorri all' alma disviata e frale,
E 'l suo difetto di tua grazia adempi!

Sì che, s' io vissi in guerra ed in tempesta,
   Mora in pace ed in porto; e se la stanza
Fu vana, almen sia la partita onesta.

A quel poco di viver che m' avanza,
Ed al morir, degni esser tua man presta:
   Tu sai ben che 'n altrui non ho speranza!

SIN.

Lord, with what care hast thou begirt us round!
    Parents first season us; then schoolmasters
Deliver us to laws; they send us bound
    To rules of reason, holy messengers;

Pulpits and Sundays, sorrow dogging sin,
    Afflictions sorted, anguish of all sizes,
Fine nets and stratagems to catch us in,
    Bibles laid open, millions of surprises;

Blessings beforehand, ties of gratefulness,
    The sound of glory ringing in our ears;
Without, our shame; within, our consciences;
    Angels and grace, eternal hopes and fears,—

    Yet all these fences, and their whole array,
    One cunning bosom-sin blows quite away!

FOR FORGIVENESS.

Wilt thou forgive that sin where I begun,
    Which was my sin, though it were done before?
Wilt thou forgive that sin through which I run,
    And do run still, though still I do deplore?
        When thou hast done, thou hast not done,
            For I have more.

Wilt thou forgive that sin which I have won
    Others to sin, and made my sin their door?
Wilt thou forgive that sin which I did shun
    A year or two, but wallowed in a score?
        When thou hast done, thou hast not done,
            For I have more.

I have a sin of fear, that when I have spun
    My last thread, I shall perish on the shore:
But swear by thyself, that at my death thy Sun
    Shall shine as he shines now, and heretofore,
        And having done that, thou hast done,—
            I fear no more.

ENTER NOT INTO JUDGMENT, O LORD!

Lord, many times I am aweary quite
    Of mine own self, my sin, my vanity;
Yet be not thou, or I am lost outright,
        Weary of me!

And hate against myself I often bear,
    And enter with myself in fierce debate:
Take thou my part against myself, nor share
        In that just hate!

Best friends might loathe us, if what things perverse
    We know of our own selves, they also knew:
Lord, Holy One! if thou, who knowest worse,
        Shouldst loathe us too!

DISCIPLINE.

Throw away thy rod,
Throw away thy wrath,
    O my God,
Take the gentle path!

For my heart's desire
Unto thine is bent:
    I aspire
To a full consent.

Though I fail, I weep:
Though I halt in pace,
    Yet I creep
To the throne of grace.

Throw away thy rod:
Though man frailties hath,
    Thou art God,—
Throw away thy wrath!

DIES IRÆ.

Dies iræ, dies illa,
Solvet sæclum in favilla,
Teste David cum Sibylla.

Quantus tremor est futurus,
Quando judex est venturus,
Cuncta stricte discussurus!

Tuba mirum spargens sonum
Per sepulcra regionum,
Coget omnes ante thronum.

Mors stupebit, et natura,
Cum resurget creatura,
Judicanti responsura.

Liber scriptus proferetur,
In quo totum continetur
Unde mundus judicetur.

DIES IRÆ.

O THAT day, that day of ire,
Told of Prophet, when in fire
Shall a world dissolved expire!

O what terror shall be then,
When the Judge shall come again,
Strictly searching deeds of men:

When a trump of awful tone,
Through the caves sepulchral blown,
Summons all before the throne.

What amazement shall o'ertake
Nature, when the dead shall wake,
Answer to the Judge to make.

Open then the book shall lie,
All o'erwrit for every eye
With a world's iniquity.

Judex ergo cum sedebit,
Quidquid latet apparebit,
Nil inultum remanebit.

Quid sum miser tunc dicturus,
Quem patronum rogaturus,
Cum vix justus sit securus!

Rex tremendæ majestatis,
Qui salvandos salvas gratis,
Salva me, fons pietatis!

Recordare, Jesu pie,
Quod sum causa tuæ viæ,
Ne me perdas illa die.

Quærens me sedisti lassus,
Redemisti crucem passus:
Tantus labor non sit cassus!

Juste judex ultionis,
Donum fac remissionis,
Ante diem rationis.

Ingemesco tanquam reus,
Culpa rubet vultus meus,
Supplicanti parce, Deus!

Dies Iræ.

When the Judge his place has ta'en,
All things hid shall be made plain,
Nothing unavenged remain.

What then, wretched! shall I speak?
Or what intercessor seek,
When the just man's cause is weak?

King of awful majesty,
Who the saved dost freely free,
Fount of mercy, pity me.

Jesus, Lord, remember, pray,
I the cause was of thy way:
Do not lose me on that day.

Tired thou satest, seeking me, —
Crucified, to set me free;
Let such pain not fruitless be.

Terrible Avenger, make
Of thy mercy me partake,
Ere that day of vengeance wake.

As a criminal I groan,
Blushing deep my fault I own:
Grace be to a suppliant shown.

Qui Mariam absolvisti,
Et latronem exaudisti,
Mihi quoque spem dedisti.

Preces meæ non sunt dignæ,
Sed tu bonus fac benigne,
Ne perenni cremer igne.

Inter oves locum præsta,
Et ab hœdis me sequestra,
Statuens in parte dextra.

Confutatis maledictis,
Flammis acribus addictis,
Voca me cum benedictis.

Oro supplex et acclinis,
Cor contritum quasi cinis;
Gere curam mei finis.

Lacrimosa dies illa,
Qua resurget ex favilla,
Judicandus homo reus:
Huic ergo parce, Deus!

Dies Iræ.

Thou who Mary didst forgive,
And who bad'st the robber live,
Hope to me dost also give.

Though my prayer unworthy be,
Yet O set me graciously
From the fire eternal free.

'Mid thy sheep my place command,
From the goats far off to stand;
Set me, Lord, at thy right hand.

And when them who scorned thee here
Thou hast judged to doom severe,
Bid me with thy saved draw near.

Lying low before thy throne,
Crushed my heart in dust, I groan;
Grace be to a suppliant shown.

UNDER THE CROSS.

I CANNOT, cannot say,
Out of my bruised and breaking heart,
Storm-driven along a thorn-set way,
While blood-drops start
From every pore, as I drag on,
"Thy will, O God, be done!"

I thought, but yesterday,
My will was one with God's dear will;
And that it would be sweet to say,
Whatever ill
My happy state should smite upon,
"Thy will, my God, be done!"

But I was weak and wrong,
Both weak of soul and wrong of heart;
And Pride alone in me was strong,
With cunning art
To cheat me in the golden sun,
To say, "God's will be done!"

Under the Cross.

O shadow drear and cold,
That frights me out of foolish pride;
O flood, that through my bosom rolled
    Its billowy tide;
I said, till ye your power made known,
    " God's will, not mine, be done!"

Now, faint and sore afraid,
Under my cross, heavy and rude,
My idols in the ashes laid,
    Like ashes strewed,
The holy words my pale lips shun,
    " O God, thy will be done!"

Pity my woes, O God,
And touch my will with thy warm breath;
Put in my trembling hand thy rod,
    That quickens death;
That my dead faith may feel thy sun,
    And say, " Thy will be done!"

NOT THIS!

What, many times I musing asked, is man,
  If grief and care
Keep far from him? he knows not what he can,
  What cannot bear.

He, till the fire hath purged him, doth remain
  Mixed all with dross:
To lack the loving discipline of pain
  Were endless loss.

Yet when my Lord did ask me on what side
  I were content
The grief whereby I must be purified,
  To me were sent,

As each imagined anguish did appear,
  Each withering bliss
Before my soul, I cried, "Oh! spare me here:
  Oh no, not this!"

Not This.

Like one that having need of, deep within,
    The surgeon's knife,
Would hardly bear that it should graze the skin,
    Though for his life.

Nay then but He, who best doth understand
    Both what we need,
And what can bear, did take my case in hand,
    Nor crying heed.

CHRIST'S CUP.

"— *And they say unto him, we can.*" — MARK x. 39.

Ah! little knew I, Lord, when thou wouldst first
Allure my trembling soul to thy dear side,
And bid me, sheltered there, in peace abide;
When I did pray as they two prayèd erst
Of thine own cup to slake their spirits' thirst,
And to sit by thee one day glorified;
Ah! little knew I how it must betide
With youth's bright hopes, and my young spirit's
      burst;
How — pale, and sad, and trembling, — I should
      see
Earth's visions, one by one, fade all away;
How this warm heart should torn and riven be,
How bitter tears should feed me night and day,
Ere on thy love my soul her all would stay,
Or walk this busy earth alone with thee.

CHASTENING.

WITHIN this leaf, to every eye
So little worth, doth hidden lie
Most rare and subtle fragrancy.

Wouldst thou its secret strength unbind?
Crush it, and thou shalt perfume find
Sweet as Arabia's spicy wind.

In this dull stone, so poor, and bare
Of shape or lustre, patient care
Will find for thee a jewel rare:

But first must skilful hands essay
With file and flint to clear away
The film which hides its fire from day.

This leaf? this stone? It is thy heart:
It must be crushed by pain and smart, —
It must be cleansed by sorrow's art, —

Ere it will yield a fragrance sweet,
Ere it will shine a jewel meet
To lay before thy dear Lord's feet.

PILGRIMAGE.

I TRAVELLED on, seeing the hill where lay
      My expectation:
A long it was and weary way:
    The gloomy Cave of Desperation
I left on the one, and on the other side
      The Rock of Pride.

And so I came to Fancy's Meadow, strowed
      With many a flower:
Fain would I here have made abode,
    But I was quickened by my hour:
So to Care's Copse I came, and there got through
      With much ado.

That led me to the Wild of Passion, which
      Some call the Wold, —
A wasted place, but sometime rich:
    Here I was robbed of all my gold,
Save one good angel, which a friend had tied
      Close to my side.

Pilgrimage.

At length I got unto the gladsome hill,
    Where lay my hope,
Where lay my heart; and climbing still,
    When I had gained the brow and top,
A lake of brackish waters on the ground
    Was all I found!

With that abashed, and struck with many a sting
    Of swarming fears,
I fell, and cried, Alas, my King!
    Can both the way and end be tears?
Yet taking heart I rose, and then perceived
    I was deceived:

My hill was further: so I flung away,
    Yet heard a cry,
Just as I went, *None goes that way
And lives.* If that be all, said I,
After so foul a journey death is fair,
    And but a chair.

PILGRIMAGE.

A PASSAGE FROM ST. AUGUSTIN.

Wert thou a wanderer on a foreign strand,
Who yet could'st only in thy native land
Find peace, or joy, or any blessed thing,—
And thy long woes unto an end to bring,
Should'st there at length determine to return,
Since in all other places doomed to mourn,—
But, having need of carriages for this,
To bring thee to thy country and true bliss,
What if the pleasant motion which they made,
With the fair prospects on each side displayed,
Should so attract thee, thou at last wert fain
The things for use lent only, to retain;
So taken with their passing, slight delight,
That, from thy country alienated quite,
And its true joys whereto thou first didst tend,
And loathing to approach thy journey's end,
Thou should'st be now a pilgrim with the fear
Lest thy long pilgrimage's close was near:
If it were this way with thee, we might say,
Thou didst man's life unto the life portray.

THE WAY IS SHORT.

I THINK we are too ready with complaint
   In this fair world of God's. Had we no hope
   Indeed beyond the zenith and the slope
Of yon gray blank of sky, we might be faint
To muse upon eternity's constraint
   Round our aspirant souls. But since the scope
   Must widen early, is it well to droop,
For a few days consumed in loss and taint?
O pusillanimous heart, be comforted,
   And, like a cheerful traveller, take the road,
Singing beside the hedge. What if the bread
   Be bitter in thine inn, and thou unshod
To meet the flints? At least it may be said,
   " Because the way is *short*, I thank thee,
      God!"

THE ANGEL OF PATIENCE.

To weary hearts, to mourning homes,
God's meekest Angel gently comes:
No power has he to banish pain,
Or give us back our lost again;
And yet, in tenderest love, our dear
And Heavenly Father sends him here.

There's quiet in that Angel's glance,
There's rest in his still countenance!
He mocks no grief with idle cheer,
Nor wounds with words the mourner's ear;
But ills and woes he may not cure
He kindly trains us to endure.

Angel of Patience! sent to calm
Our feverish brows with cooling palm;
To lay the storms of hope and fear,
And reconcile life's smile and tear;
The throbs of wounded grief to still,
And make our own our Father's will!

The Angel of Patience.

O thou who mournest on thy way,
With longings for the close of day,
He walks with thee, that Angel kind,
And gently whispers, " Be resigned :
Bear up, bear on, the end shall tell
The dear Lord ordereth all things well ! "

VIA CRUCIS VIA LUCIS.

Through night to light! And though to mortal eyes
  Creation's face a pall of horror wear,
Good cheer! good cheer! The gloom of midnight flies;
  Then shall a sunrise follow, mild and fair.

Through storm to calm! And though his thunder-car
  The rumbling tempest drive through earth and sky,
Good cheer! good cheer! The elemental war
  Tells that a blessed, healing hour is nigh.

Through frost to spring! And though the biting blast
  Of Eurus stiffen nature's juicy veins,
Good cheer! good cheer! When winter's wrath is past,
  Soft-murmuring spring breathes sweetly o'er the plains.

Via Crucis via Lucis.

Through strife to peace! And though, with bristling front,
 A thousand frightful deaths encompass thee,
Good cheer! good cheer! brave thou the battle's brunt
 For the peace-march and song of victory.

Through toil to sleep! And though the sultry noon,
 With heavy, drooping wing, oppress thee now,
Good cheer! good cheer! the cool of evening soon
 Shall lull to sweet repose thy weary brow.

Through cross to crown! And though thy spirit's life
 Trials untold assail with giant strength,
Good cheer! good cheer! soon ends the bitter strife,
 And thou shalt reign in peace with Christ at length.

Through woe to joy! And though at morn thou weep,
 And though the midnight find thee weeping still,
Good cheer! good cheer! the Shepherd loves his sheep;
 Resign thee to the watchful Father's will.

THROUGH DEATH TO LIFE! And through this
    vale of tears,
And through this thistle-field of life, ascend
To the great supper, in that world whose years
    Of bliss unfading, cloudless, know no end.

ΠΑΘΕΙ ΜΑΘΟΣ.

I ONLY would be spent, — in pain
And loss, perchance, — but not in vain.

I am content to be so weak, —
Put strength into the words I speak,
And I am strong in what I seek!

I am content to be so bare
Before the archers; everywhere
My wounds being stroked by heavenly air.

Because my portion was assigned
Wholesome and bitter — thou art kind,
And I am blessed to my mind.

I KNOW — is all the mourner saith:
Knowledge by suffering entereth,
And Life is perfected by Death!

Glory to God — to God! he saith:
KNOWLEDGE BY SUFFERING entereth,
And Life is perfected by Death!

ADVERSA MUNDI TOLERA.

Adversa mundi tolera
Pro Christi nomine;
Plus nocent sæpe prospera
Cum levi flamine.

Quum a multis molestaris,
Nihil perdis, sed lucraris;
Patiendo promereris,
Multa bona consequeris.

Nam Deum honorificas,
Et angelos lætificas;
Coronam tuam duplicas,
Et proximos ædificas.

Labor parvus est et brevis vita,
Merces grandis est, quies infinita;
Toties martyr Dei efficeris,
Quoties pro Deo pœnam patieris.

ENDURE THE WORLD'S RUDE BUFFETINGS.

ENDURE the world's rude buffetings,
For Christ and Charity;
More hurtful oft the flatterings
Of mild prosperity.

When much wrong thy soul endureth,
Gain, not loss, to thee inureth;
Patience rich reward insureth,
Goods full many it procureth.

For thou the Lord dost glorify,
And joys of angels multiply;
A twofold crown thou winn'st thereby,
And dost thy neighbors edify.

Light the labor, — earthly life soon speedeth;
Great the gain, — eternal rest succeedeth;
Martyr of God, so oft a crown thou wearest
As for God a martyr's pang thou bearest.

Patiendo fit homo melior,
Auro pulchrior, vitro clarior,
A vitiis purgatior,
Virtutibus perfectior:

Jesu Christo acceptior,
Sanctis quoque similior,
Hostibus suis fortior,
Amicis amabilior.

By patience man becomes more excellent,
Fairer than gold, clear as the firmament,
More pure from each vile element,
In every grace more eminent:

To Jesus more acceptable,
More like to saints unblamable,
To enemies more terrible,
And to his friends more lovable.

A CITY THAT HATH FOUNDATIONS.

. . . .

Therefore, O friend, I would not, if I might,
   Rebuild my house of lies, wherein I joyed
One time to dwell: my soul shall walk in white,
   Cast down, but not destroyed.

Therefore in patience I possess my soul;
   Yea, therefore as a flint I set my face,
To pluck down, to build up again the whole, —
   But in a distant place.

These thorns are sharp, yet I can tread on them;
   This cup is loathsome, yet He makes it sweet;
My face is steadfast toward Jerusalem,
   My heart remembers it,

I lift the hanging hands, the feeble knees, —
   I, precious more than seven times molten
      gold, —
Until the day when from his storehouses
   God shall bring new and old;

Beauty for ashes, oil of joy for grief,
    Garment of praise for spirit of heaviness;
Although to-day I fade as doth a leaf,
    I languish and grow less.

Although to-day he prunes my twigs with pain,
    Yet doth his blood nourish and warm my root:
To-morrow I shall put forth buds again,
    And clothe myself with fruit.

Although to-day I walk in tedious ways,
    To-day his staff is turned into a rod, —
Yet will I wait for him the appointed days,
    And stay upon my God.

"REJOICE EVERMORE."

    But how should we be glad?
We, that are journeying through a vale of tears,
Encompast with a thousand woes and fears,
    How should we not be sad?

    Angels that ever stand
Within the presence-chamber, and there raise
The never-interrupted hymn of praise,
    May welcome this command.

    Or they whose strife is o'er,
Who all their weary length of life have trod,
As pillars now within the temple of God,
    That shall go out no more.

    But we, who wander here,
We that are exiled in this gloomy place,
Still doomed to water earth's unthankful face
    With many a bitter tear, —

"Rejoice Evermore."

Bid us lament and mourn,
Bid us that we go mourning all the day,
And we will find it easy to obey,
    Of our best things forlorn.

But not that we be glad;
If it be true the mourners are the blest,
O leave us, in a world of sin, unrest,
    And trouble, to be sad.

I spake, and thought to weep;
For sin and sorrow, suffering and crime,
That fill the world, all mine appointed time
    A settled grief to keep.

When lo! as day from night,
As day from out the womb of night forlorn,
So from that sorrow was that gladness born,
    Even in mine own despite.

Yet was not that by this
Excluded; at the coming of that joy
Fled not that grief, nor did that grief destroy
    The newly-risen bliss:

But side by side they flow,
Two fountains flowing from one smitten heart,

And ofttimes scarcely to be known apart, —
  That gladness and that woe.

Two fountains from one source,
Or which from two such neighboring sources run,
That aye for him who shall unseal the one,
  The other flows perforce.

And both are sweet and calm;
Fair flowers upon the banks of either blow;
Both fertilize the soil, and where they flow
  Shed round them holy balm.

TO SORROW.

Sister Sorrow! sit beside me,
Or, if I must wander, guide me:
Let me take thy hand in mine;
Cold alike are mine and thine.

Think not, Sorrow, that I hate thee;
Think not I am frightened at thee;
Thou art come for some good end,
I will treat thee as a friend.

I will say that thou art bound
My unshielded soul to wound
By some force without thy will,
And art tender-minded still.

I will say thou givest scope
To the breath and light of hope;
That thy gentle tears have weight
Hardest hearts to penetrate;

That thy shadow brings together
Friends long lost in sunny weather,
With an hundred offices
Beautiful and blest as these.

Softly takest thou the crown
From my haughty temples down :
Place it on thine own pale brow ;
Pleasure wears one, — why not thou ?

Let the blossoms glitter there
On thy long unbanded hair,
And, when I have borne my pain,
Thou wilt give me them again.

SAD AND SWEET.

Sad is our youth, for it is ever going,
Crumbling away beneath our very feet:
Sad is our life, for it is ever flowing,
In current unperceived, because so fleet:
Sad are our hopes, for they were sweet in sowing,
But tares self-sown have overtopped the wheat:
Sad are our joys, for they were sweet in blowing,
And still, O still their dying breath is sweet.
And sweet is youth, although it hath bereft us
Of that which made our childhood sweeter still;
And sweet is middle life, for it hath left us
A newer Good to cure an older Ill:
And sweet are all things, when we learn to prize them,
Not for their sake, but His who grants them, or denies them!

LOVE AND DISCIPLINE.

Since in a land not barren still,
Because thou dost thy grace distil,
My lot is fall'n, blest be thy will!

And since these biting frosts but kill
Some tares in me, which choke or spill
That seed thou sow'st, blest be thy skill!

Blest be thy dew, and blest thy frost,
And happy I to be so crost,
And cured by crosses at thy cost.

The dew doth cheer what is distrest;
The frosts ill weeds nip and molest;
In both thou work'st unto the best.

THEY ARE ALL GONE.

They are all gone into the world of light,
    And I alone sit lingering here!
Their very memory is fair and bright,
    And my sad thoughts doth clear.

It glows and glitters in my cloudy breast
    Like stars upon some gloomy grove,
Or those faint beams in which this hill is drest
    After the sun's remove.

I see them walking in an air of glory,
    Whose light doth trample on my days, —
My days, which are at best but dull and hoary,
    Mere glimmering and decays.

O holy hope, and high humility!
    High as the heavens above!
These are your walks, and you have showed them me
    To kindle my cold love.

Dear, beauteous Death, the jewel of the just,
    Shining nowhere but in the dark,
What mysteries do lie beyond thy dust,
    Could man outlook that mark!

He that hath found some fledged bird's nest may know
    At first sight if the bird be flown;
But what fair dell or grove he sings in now —
    That is to him unknown.

And yet, as angels, in some brighter dreams,
    Call to the soul when man doth sleep,
So some strange thoughts transcend our wonted themes,
    And into glory peep.

If a star were confined into a tomb,
    Her captive flames must needs burn there;
But when the hand that locked her up gives room,
    She'll shine through all the sphere.

O Father of eternal life, and all
    Created glories under thee,
Resume thy spirit from this world of thrall
    Into true liberty!

Either disperse these mists, which blot and fill
    My perspective still as they pass ;
Or else remove me hence unto that hill
    Where I shall need no glass.

VANISHED.

The voice which I did more esteem
   Than music in her sweetest key, —
Those eyes which unto me did seem
   More comfortable than the day, —
Those now by me, as they have been,
Shall never more be heard or seen;
But what I once enjoyed in them
Shall seem hereafter as a dream.

All earthly comforts vanish thus;
   So little hold of them have we,
That we from them, or they from us,
   May in a moment ravished be.
Yet we are neither just nor wise
If present mercies we despise;
Or mind not how there may be made
A thankful use of what we had.

DE PROFUNDIS.

The face which, duly as the sun,
Rose up for me with life begun,
To mark all bright hours of the day
With hourly love, is dimmed away, —
And yet my days go on, — go on.

The heart which, like a staff, was one
For mine to lean and rest upon,
The strongest on the longest day
With steadfast love, is caught away, —
And yet my days go on, — go on.

And cold before my summer's done,
And deaf in Nature's general tune,
And fallen too low for special fear,
And here, with hope no longer here, —
While the tears drop, my days go on.

Breath freezes on my lips to moan:
As one alone — once not alone —

I sit and knock at Nature's door,
Heart-bare, heart-hungry, very poor,
Whose desolated days go on.

I knock, and cry, Undone, undone!
Is there no help, no comfort, — none?
No gleaning in the wide wheat-plains
Where others drive their loaded wains?
My vacant days go on, — go on.

— A Voice reproves me thereupon,
More sweet than Nature's when the drone
Of bees is sweetest, and more deep
Than when the rivers overleap
The shuddering pines, and thunder on.

God's Voice, not Nature's: night and noon
He sits upon the great white throne,
And listens for the creatures' praise.
What babble we of days and days?
The Day-spring He, whose days go on.

He reigns above, he reigns alone;
Systems burn out and leave his throne;
Fair mists of seraphs melt and fall
Around him, changeless amid all, —
Ancient of Days, whose days go on.

De Profundis.

By anguish which made pale the sun,
I hear him charge his saints that none
Among his creatures, anywhere,
Blaspheme against him with despair,
However darkly days go on.

For us, whatever's undergone,
Thou knowest, willest what is done.
Grief may be joy misunderstood;
Only the Good discerns the good:
I trust thee while my days go on.

I praise thee while my days go on;
I love thee while my days go on:
Through dark and dearth, through fire and frost,
With emptied arms and treasure lost,
I thank thee while my days go on.

THE TWO ANGELS.

Two angels, one of Life and one of Death,
    Passed o'er our village as the morning broke;
The dawn was on their faces, and beneath,
    The sombre houses hearsed with plumes of smoke,

Their attitude and aspect were the same,
    Alike their features and their robes of white;
But one was crowned with amaranth, as with flame,
    And one with asphodels, like flakes of light.

I saw them pause on their celestial way;
    Then said I, with deep fear and doubt opprest,
" Beat not so loud, my heart, lest thou betray
    The place where thy beloved are at rest!"

And he who wore the crown of asphodels,
    Descending, at my door began to knock,
And my soul sank within me, as in wells
    The waters sink before an earthquake's shock.

I recognized the nameless agony,
  The terror and the tremor and the pain,
That oft before had filled or haunted me,
  And now returned with threefold strength again.

The door I opened to my heavenly guest,
  And listened, for I thought I heard God's voice;
And, knowing whatsoe'er he sent was best,
  Dared neither to lament nor to rejoice.

Then with a smile, that filled the house with light,
  "My errand is not Death, but Life," he said;
And ere I answered, passing out of sight.
  On his celestial embassy he sped.

'T was at thy door, O friend! and not at mine,
  The angel with the amaranthine wreath,
Pausing, descended, and with voice divine,
  Whispered a word that had a sound like Death.

Then fell upon the house a sudden gloom,
  A shadow on those features fair and thin;
And softly, from that hushed and darkened room,
  Two angels issued, where but one went in.

All is of God! If he but wave his hand,
    The mists collect, the rain falls thick and loud
Till, with a smile of light on sea and land,
    Lo! he looks back from the departing cloud.

Angels of Life and Death alike are his;
    Without his leave they pass no threshold o'er;
Who, then, would wish, or dare, believing this,
    Against his messengers to shut the door?

RESIGNATION.

There is no flock, however watched and tended,
  But one dead lamb is there!
There is no fireside, howsoe'er defended,
  But has one vacant chair!

The air is full of farewells to the dying,
  And mournings for the dead;
The heart of Rachel, for her children crying,
  Will not be comforted!

Let us be patient! These severe afflictions
  Not from the ground arise,
But oftentimes celestial benedictions
  Assume this dark disguise.

We see but dimly through the mists and vapors;
  Amid these earthly damps
What seem to us but sad, funereal tapers
  May be heaven's distant lamps.

There is no Death! What seems so is transition:
  This life of mortal breath
Is but a suburb of the life elysian,
  Whose portal we call Death.

She is not dead, — the child of our affection, —
  But gone unto that school
Where she no longer needs our poor protection,
  And Christ himself doth rule.

In that great cloister's stillness and seclusion,
  By guardian angels led,
Safe from temptation, safe from sin's pollution,
  She lives, whom we call dead.

Day after day we think what she is doing
  In those bright realms of air;
Year after year, her tender steps pursuing,
  Behold her grown more fair.

Thus do we walk with her, and keep unbroken
  The bond which nature gives,
Thinking that our remembrance, though unspoken,
  May reach her where she lives.

Not as a child shall we again behold her;
  For when with raptures wild

In our embraces we again enfold her,
  She will not be a child:

But a fair maiden, in her Father's mansion,
  Clothed with celestial grace;
And beautiful with all the soul's expansion
  Shall we behold her face.

And though, at times, impetuous with emotion
  And anguish long suppressed,
The swelling heart heaves moaning like the ocean,
  That cannot be at rest,—

We will be patient, and assuage the feeling
  We may not wholly stay;
By silence sanctifying, not concealing,
  The grief that must have way.

THE ALPINE SHEEP.

When on my ear your loss was knelled,
    And tender sympathy upburst,
A little spring from memory welled,
    Which once had quenched my bitter thirst.

And I was fain to bear to you
    A portion of its mild relief,
That it might be as cooling dew,
    To steal some fever from your grief.

After our child's untroubled breath
    Up to the Father took its way,
And on our home the shade of death
    Like a long twilight haunting lay,

And friends came round, with us to weep
    Her little spirit's swift remove,
The story of the Alpine sheep
    Was told to us by one we love.

The Alpine Sheep.

They, in the valley's sheltering care,
   Soon crop the meadow's tender prime,
And when the sod grows brown and bare,
   The shepherd strives to make them climb

To airy shelves of pasture green,
   That hang along the mountain's side,
Where grass and flowers together lean,
   And down through mists the sunbeams slide.

But nought can tempt the timid things
   The steep and rugged path to try,
Though sweet the shepherd calls and sings,
   And seared below the pastures lie, —

Till in his arms their lambs he takes,
   Along the dizzy verge to go.
Then, heedless of the rifts and breaks,
   They follow on, o'er rock and snow.

And in those pastures, lifted fair,
   More dewy soft than lowland mead,
The shepherd drops his tender care,
   And sheep and lambs together feed.

This parable, by Nature breathed,
   Blew on me as the south wind free
O'er frozen brooks, that flow unsheathed
   From icy thraldom to the sea.

A blissful vision, through the night,
  Would all my happy senses sway,
Of the Good Shepherd on the height,
  Or climbing up the starry way,

Holding *our* little lamb asleep, —
  While, like the murmur of the sea,
Sounded that voice along the deep,
  Saying, " Arise, and follow me!"

DEAR FRIEND, FAR OFF, MY LOST DESIRE.

Dear friend, far off, my lost desire,
    So far, so near, in woe and weal;
    Oh, loved the most when most I feel
There is a lower and a higher:

Known and unknown, — human, divine!
    Sweet human hand and lips and eye,
    Dear heavenly friend that canst not die,
Mine, mine forever, ever mine!

Strange friend, — past, present, and to be,
    Loved deeplier, darklier understood;
    Behold I dream a dream of good,
And mingle all the world with thee.

Thy voice is on the rolling air;
    I hear thee where the waters run;
    Thou standest in the rising sun,
And in the setting thou art fair.

What art thou, then? I cannot guess;
 But though I seem in star and flower
 To feel thee, some diffusive power,
I do not therefore love thee less.

Far off thou art, but ever nigh;
 I have thee still, and I rejoice;
 I prosper, circled with thy voice;
I shall not lose thee, though I die.

THE PAST.

Thou unrelenting Past!
Strong are the barriers round thy dark domain,
    And fetters, sure and fast,
Hold all that enter thy unbreathing reign.

    Far in thy realm withdrawn,
Old empires sit in sullenness and gloom,
    And glorious ages gone
Lie deep within the shadow of thy womb.

    Childhood, with all its mirth,
Youth, Manhood, Age, that draws us to the ground,
    And last, Man's Life on earth,
Glide to thy dim dominions, and are bound.

    Thou hast my better years,
Thou hast my earlier friends, the good, the kind,
    Yielded to thee with tears, —
The venerable form, the exalted mind.

The Past.

    My spirit yearns to bring
The lost ones back,— yearns with desire intense,
    And struggles hard to wring
Thy bolts apart, and pluck thy captives thence.

    In vain: thy gates deny
All passage save to those who hence depart;
    Nor to the streaming eye
Thou giv'st them back, nor to the broken heart.

    In thy abysses hide
Beauty and excellence unknown; to thee
    Earth's wonder and her pride
Are gathered, as the waters to the sea;

    Labors of good to man,
Unpublished charity, unbroken faith;
    Love, that midst grief began,
And grew with years, and faltered not in death.

    Full many a mighty name
Lurks in thy depths, unuttered, unrevered;
    With thee are silent fame,
Forgotten arts, and wisdom disappeared.

    Thine for a space are they:
Yet shalt thou yield thy treasures up at last;
    Thy gates shall yet give way,
Thy bolts shall fall, inexorable Past!

The Past.

All that of good and fair
Has gone into thy womb from earliest time,
    Shall then come forth to wear
The glory and the beauty of its prime.

    They have not perished; no!
Kind words, remembered voices once so sweet,
    Smiles, radiant long ago,
And features, the great soul's apparent seat,—

    All shall come back : each tie
Of pure affection shall be knit again ;
    Alone shall Evil die,
And Sorrow dwell a prisoner in thy reign.

    And then shall I behold
Him, by whose kind paternal side I sprung,
    And her, who, still and cold,
Fills the next grave,— the beautiful and young.

FOOTSTEPS OF ANGELS.

When the hours of day are numbered,
    And the voices of the night
Wake the better soul, that slumbered,
    To a holy, calm delight;

Ere the evening lamps are lighted,
    And, like phantoms grim and tall,
Shadows from the fitful firelight
    Dance upon the parlor wall;

Then the forms of the departed
    Enter at the open door;
The beloved, the true-hearted,
    Come to visit me once more.

He, the young and strong, who cherished
    Noble longings for the strife,
By the roadside fell and perished,
    Weary with the march of life.

Footsteps of Angels.

They. the holy ones and weakly,
    Who the cross of suffering bore,
Folded their pale hands so meekly,
    Spake with us on earth no more.

And with them the being beauteous,
    Who unto my youth was given,
More than all things else to love me,
    And is now a saint in heaven.

With a slow and noiseless footstep
    Comes that messenger divine,
Takes the vacant chair beside me,
    Lays her gentle hand in mine.

And she sits and gazes at me
    With those deep and tender eyes,
Like the stars, so still and saintlike,
    Looking downward from the skies.

Uttered not, yet comprehended,
    Is the spirit's voiceless prayer,
Soft rebukes, in blessings ended,
    Breathing from her lips of air.

Oh, though oft depressed and lonely,
    All my fears are laid aside,
If I but remember only
    Such as these have lived and died!

AN ANGEL IN THE HOUSE.

How sweet it were if, without feeble fright,
Or dying of the dreadful beauteous sight,
An angel came to us, and we could bear
To see him issue from the silent air
At evening in our room, and bend on ours
His divine eyes, and bring us from his bowers
News of dear friends, and children who have never
Been dead indeed, — as we shall know forever.
Alas! we think not what we daily see
About our hearths, angels, that *are* to be,
Or may be if they will, and we prepare
Their souls and ours to meet in happy air, —
A child, a friend, a wife whose soft heart sings
In unison with ours, breeding its future wings.

BE NEAR ME WHEN MY LIGHT IS LOW.

Be near me when my light is low,
　When the blood creeps, and the nerves prick
　And tingle ; and the heart is sick,
And all the wheels of Being slow.

Be near me when the sensuous frame
　Is racked with pangs that conquer trust ;
　And Time, a maniac scattering dust,
And Life, a Fury slinging flame.

Be near me when my faith is dry,
　And men the flies of latter spring,
　That lay their eggs, and sting and sing,
And weave their petty cells, and die.

Be near me when I fade away,
　To point the term of human strife,
　And on the low dark verge of life
The twilight of eternal day.

DO WE INDEED DESIRE THE DEAD?

Do we indeed desire the dead
   Should still be near us at our side?
   Is there no baseness we would hide?
No inner vileness that we dread?

Shall he for whose applause I strove,—
   I had such reverence for his blame,—
   See with clear eyes some hidden shame,
And I be lessened in his love?

I wrong the grave with fears untrue:
   Shall love be blamed for want of faith?
   There must be wisdom with great Death:
The dead shall look me through and through.

Be near us when we climb or fall:
   Ye watch, like God, the rolling hours
   With larger, other eyes than ours,
To make allowance for us all.

— *Not for that we would be unclothed, but clothed upon, that mortality might be swallowed up of life.* — 2 COR. ii. 4.

In health, O Lord, and prosperous days,
When worldly wealth or worldly praise,
When worldly thoughts have filled our heart,
We would not from the body part;
And then the very thought is loathed,
That we must be by death unclothed.

In sickness, sorrow, or in shame,
We fain would quit this mortal frame;
But thus to shrink from toil and pain,
This is not longing for thy reign:
Brought low, we only seek to be
Unclothed, not clothed upon by thee.

O rather help us as we ought
To feel what thine Apostle taught, —
That not for aye we seek to wear
This form of clay, corruption's heir,
Nor yet impatient ask alone
To be unclothed, but clothed upon!

THE SICK ROOM.

Watching, through the silent hours,
   By the unrefreshèd bed,
Where disease arrays his powers,
   Whence repose is banishèd,
Where time halteth, sad and slow,
Thou art with me, Lord, I know.

When the vital forces seem
   Dwindled to as faint a spark
As the taper's sickly gleam,
   Making darkness doubly dark, —
Lord! I bless thee that thou art
Near, to stay the sinking heart.

When the flame, reviving, burns
   Gently, and at sleep's soft touch
Anguish yields, and hope returns,
   Dove-like, to the smoothèd couch, —
With an anxious deep-drawn sigh,
Lord, I praise thee, ever nigh.

The Sick Room.

In the dim religious gloom,
  Where 'expressive silence' broods
O'er the closely curtained room,
  Nor a stirring breath intrudes,—
As in silent prayer I kneel,
Thou art present, Lord, I feel.

When reluctant hope is fled,
  When the pulses beat no more,
And the last farewell is said,
  And the war of life is o'er,—
Lord, both the spirit and the dust
Of our beloved, to thee we trust.

WHOLESOME MEMORIES OF PAIN.

Who that a watcher doth remain
Beside a couch of mortal pain,
Deems he can ever smile again?

Or who that weeps beside a bier,
Counts he has any more to fear
From the world's flatteries, false and leer?

And yet anon, and he doth start
At the light toys in which his heart
Can now already claim its part.

O hearts of ours, so weak and poor,
That nothing there can long endure!
And so their hurts find shameful cure;

While every sadder, wiser thought,
Each holier aim which sorrow brought,
Fades quite away and comes to nought.

O Thou who dost our weakness know,
Watch for us, that the strong hours so
Not wean us from our wholesome woe.

Grant thou that we may long retain
The wholesome memories of pain,
Nor wish to lose them soon again.

THE DAY OF DEATH.

Thou inevitable day,
When a voice to me shall say,
" Thou must rise and come away;

" All thine other journeys past,
Gird thee, and make ready fast
For thy longest and thy last;" —

Day deep-hidden from our sight
In impenetrable night,
Who may guess of thee aright?

Art thou distant, art thou near?
Wilt thou seem more dark or clear?
Day with more of hope or fear?

Wilt thou come, not seen before
Thou art standing at the door,
Saying — Light and life are o'er?

The Day of Death.

Or with such a gradual pace
As shall leave me largest space
To regard thee face to face?

Shall I lay my drooping head
On some loved lap; round my bed
Prayer be made, and tears be shed?

Or at distance from mine own,
Name and kin alike unknown,
Make my solitary moan?

Will there yet be things to leave,
Hearts to which this heart must cleave,
From which, parting, it must grieve;

Or shall life's best ties be o'er,
And all loved things gone before
To that other happier shore?

Shall I gently fall on sleep,
Death, like slumber, o'er me creep,
Like a slumber sweet and deep?

Or the soul long strive in vain
To get free, with toil and pain,
From its half-divided chain?

Little skills it where or how,
If thou comest then or now,
With a smooth or angry brow;

Come thou must, and we must die:
Jesus, Saviour, stand thou by,
When that last sleep seals our eye.

THE CLOUD ON THE WAY.

See before us in our journey broods a mist upon
    the ground;
Thither leads the path we walk in, blending with
    that gloomy bound:
Never eye hath pierced its shadows to the mys-
    tery they screen;
Those who once have passed within it never
    more on earth are seen.
Now it seems to stoop beside us, now at seeming
    distance lowers,
Leaving banks that tempt us onward bright with
    summer-green and flowers:
Yet it blots the way forever; there our journey
    ends at last;
Into that dark cloud we enter, and are gathered
    to the past.

Thou who, in this flinty pathway, leading through
    a stranger-land,
Passest down the rocky valley, walking with me
    hand-in-hand,

Which of us shall be the soonest folded to that
    dim Unknown?
Which shall leave the other walking in this flinty
    path alone?
Even now I see thee shudder, and thy cheek is
    white with fear,
And thou clingest to my side as comes that dark-
    ness sweeping near.
"Here," thou sayst, "the path is rugged, sown
    with thorns that wound the feet;
But the sheltered glens are lovely, and the rivu-
    let's song is sweet;
Roses breathe from tangled thickets; lilies bend
    from ledges brown;
Pleasantly between the pelting showers the sun-
    shine gushes down;
Dear are those who walk beside us, they whose
    looks and voices make
All this rugged region cheerful, till I love it for
    their sake.
Far be yet the hour that takes me where that
    chilly shadow lies,
From the things I know and love, and from the
    sight of loving eyes."

So thou murmurest, fearful one: but see, we
    tread a rougher way;
Fainter glow the gleams of sunshine that upon
    the dark rocks play;

The Cloud on the Way.

Rude winds strew the faded flowers upon the
    crags o'er which we pass;
Banks of verdure, when we reach them, hiss with
    tufts of withered grass.
One by one we miss the voices which we loved
    so well to hear;
One by one the kindly faces in that shadow dis-
    appear.

Yet upon the mist before us fix thine eyes with
    closer view:
See, beneath its sullen skirts, the rosy morning
    glimmers through.
One whose feet the thorns have wounded, passed
    that barrier and came back,
With a glory on his footsteps lighting yet the
    dreary track.
Boldly enter where He entered; all that seems
    but darkness here,
When thou once hast passed beyond it, haply
    shall be crystal-clear.
Viewed from that serener realm, the walks of
    human life may lie,
Like the page of some familiar volume, open to
    thine eye;
Haply, from the overhanging shadow, thou mayst
    stretch an unseen hand,
To support the wavering steps that paint with
    blood the rugged land.

Haply, leaning o'er the pilgrim, all unweeting
 thou art near,
Thou mayst whisper words of warning or of
 comfort in his ear,
Till, beyond the border where that brooding
 mystery bars the sight,
Those whom thou hast fondly cherished stand
 with thee in peace and light.

THE BORDER-LANDS.

Father, into thy loving hands
    My feeble spirit I commit,
While wandering in these Border-Lands
    Until thy voice shall summon it.

Father, I would not dare to choose
    A longer life, an earlier death;
I know not what my soul might lose
    By shortened or protracted breath.

These Border-Lands are calm and still,
    And solemn are their silent shades;
And my heart welcomes them, until
    The light of life's long evening fades.

I heard them spoken of with dread,
    As fearful and unquiet places, —
Shades, where the living and the dead
    Look sadly in each other's faces.

But since thy hand hath led me here,
    And I have seen the Border-Land, —
Seen the dark river flowing near,
    Stood on its brink, as now I stand, —

There has been nothing to alarm
    My trembling soul; how could I fear
While thus encircled with thine arm?
    I never felt thee half so near.

What should appall me in a place
    That brings me hourly nearer thee? —
When I may almost see thy face!
    Surely 't is here my soul would be.

They say the waves are dark and deep,
    That faith has perished in the river;
They speak of death with fear, and weep.
    Shall my soul perish? Never, never!

I know that thou wilt never leave
    The soul that trembles while it clings
To thee: I know thou wilt achieve
    Its passage on thine outspread wings.

And since I first was brought so near
    The stream that flows to the Dead Sea,
I think that it has grown more clear
    And shallow than it used to be.

The Border-Lands.

I cannot see the golden gate
  Unfolding yet to welcome me;
I cannot yet anticipate
  The joy of heaven's jubilee.

But I will calmly watch and pray,
  Until I hear my Saviour's voice,
Calling my happy soul away
  To see his glory, and rejoice.

THE TRUE LIGHT.

To thee, to all, my sinking voice,
   Beloved! would fain once more proclaim,
In Christ alone may those rejoice
   Deceived by every other name.

In all but Him our sins have been,
   And wanderings dark of doubtful mind;
In Him alone on earth is seen
   God's perfect will for all mankind.

The shadows round me close and press,
   But still that radiant orb I see,
And more I seem its light to bless
   Than aught near worlds could give to me.

As light and warmth to noontide hours,
   To sweetest voices tuneful songs,
And as to summer fields the flowers,
   So heaven to heavenly souls belongs.

DUST TO DUST.

On blessing, wearing semblance of a curse,
   We fear thee, thou stern sentence; yet to be
Linked to immortal bodies, were far worse
      Than thus to be set free.

For mingling with the life-blood, through each vein
   The venom of the Serpent's bite has run,
And only thus might be expelled again, —
      Thus only health be won.

Shall we not then a gracious sentence own,
   Now since the leprosy has fretted through
The entire house, that Thou wilt take it down,
      And build it all anew?

Build it this time, since Thou wilt build again,
   An holy house where righteousness may dwell;
And we, though in the unbuilding there be pain,
      Will still affirm, — 'T is well.

THE ILLUSION OF LIFE.

MYSTERIOUS Night! when our first parent knew
  Thee, from report divine, and heard thy name,
  Did he not tremble for this lovely frame,
This glorious canopy of light and blue?
Yet 'neath a curtain of translucent dew,
  Bathed in the rays of the great setting flame,
  Hesperus with the host of heaven came,
And lo! creation widened in man's view.
Who could have thought such darkness lay concealed
  Within thy beams, O Sun? or who could find,
Whilst fly and leaf and insect stood revealed,
  That to such countless orbs thou mad'st us blind?
Why do we, then, shun death with anxious strife?
If light can thus deceive, wherefore not life?

THE FUTURE LIFE.

How shall I know thee in the sphere which keeps
   The disembodied spirits of the dead,
When all of thee that time could wither sleeps,
   And perishes among the dust we tread?

For I shall feel the sting of ceaseless pain,
   If there I meet thy gentle presence not;
Nor hear the voice I love, nor read again
   In thy serenest eyes the tender thought.

Will not thy own meek heart demand me there?
   That heart whose fondest throbs to me were given?
My name on earth was ever in thy prayer,
   And must thou never utter it in heaven?

In meadows fanned by heaven's life-breathing wind,
   In the resplendence of that glorious sphere,
And larger movements of the unfettered mind,
   Wilt thou forget the love that joined us here?

The love that lived through all the stormy past,
  And meekly with my harsher nature bore,
And deeper grew, and tenderer to the last,
  Shall it expire with life, and be no more?

A happier lot than mine, and larger light,
  Await thee there; for thou hast bowed thy will
In cheerful homage to the rule of right,
  And lovest all, and renderest good for ill.

For me, the sordid cares in which I dwell
  Shrink and consume my heart, as heat the scroll;
And wrath has left its scar, — that fire of hell
  Has left its frightful scar upon my soul.

Yet though thou wear'st the glory of the sky,
  Wilt thou not keep the same beloved name,
The same fair thoughtful brow, and gentle eye,
  Lovelier in heaven's sweet climate, yet the same?

Shalt thou not teach me, in that calmer home,
  The wisdom that I learned so ill in this, —
The wisdom which is love, — till I become
  Thy fit companion in that land of bliss?

THE RETURN OF YOUTH.

My friend, thou sorrowest for thy golden prime,
    For thy fair youthful years, too swift of flight;
Thou musest, with wet eyes, upon the time
    Of cheerful hopes that filled the world with light,—
Years when thy heart was bold, thy hand was strong,
    And quick the thought that moved thy tongue to speak,
And willing faith was thine, and scorn of wrong
    Summoned the sudden crimson to thy cheek.

Thou lookest forward on the coming days,
    Shuddering to feel their shadow o'er thee creep;
A path, thick-set with changes and decays,
    Slopes downward to the place of common sleep;
And they who walked with thee in life's first stage
    Leave one by one thy side, and, waiting near,

Thou seest the sad companions of thy age, —
    Dull love of rest, and weariness, and fear.

Yet grieve thou not, nor think thy youth is gone,
    Nor deem that glorious season e'er could die;
Thy pleasant youth, a little while withdrawn,
    Waits on the horizon of a brighter sky;
Waits, like the morn, that folds her wing and hides,
    Till the slow stars bring back her dawning hour;
Waits, like the vanished spring, that slumbering bides
    Her own sweet time to waken bud and flower.

There shall he welcome thee, when thou shalt stand
    On his bright morning hills, with smiles more sweet
Than when at first he took thee by the hand,
    Through the fair earth to lead thy tender feet.
He shall bring back, but brighter, broader still,
    Life's early glory to thine eyes again, —
Shall clothe thy spirit with new strength, and fill
    Thy leaping heart with warmer love than then.

Hast thou not glimpses, in the twilight here,
    Of mountains where immortal morn prevails?

Comes there not, through the silence, to thine
    ear
A gentle rustling of the morning gales?
A murmur, wafted from that glorious shore,
    Of streams that water banks forever fair,
And voices of the loved ones gone before,
    More musical in that celestial air?

SUBMISSION.

Thy will be done! I will not fear
    The fate provided by thy love;
Though clouds and darkness shroud me here,
    I know that all is bright above.

The stars of heaven are shining on,
    Though these frail eyes are dimmed with tears;
And though the hopes of earth be gone,
    Yet are not ours the immortal years?

Father! forgive the heart that clings,
    Thus trembling, to the things of time;
And bid the soul, on angel wings,
    Ascend into a purer clime.

There shall no doubts disturb its trust,
    No sorrows dim celestial love;
But these afflictions of the dust,
    Like shadows of the night, remove.

WORK.

Thou hast, midst Life's empty noises,
   Heard the solemn steps of Time,
And the low mysterious voices
   Of another clime.

All the mystery of Being
   Hath upon thy spirit pressed;
Thoughts which, like the deluge-wanderer,
   Find no place of rest.

From the doubt and darkness springing
   Of the dim, uncertain Past,
Moving to the dark still shadows
   O'er the Future cast,

Early hath Life's mighty question
   Thrilled within thy heart of youth,
With a deep and strong beseeching,—
   What, and where, is Truth?

And to thee an answer cometh
  From the earth and from the sky,
And to thee the hills and waters,
  And the stars reply.

But a soul-sufficing answer
  Hath no outward origin;
More than Nature's many voices
  May be heard within.

Not to ease and aimless quiet
  Doth that inward answer tend;
But to works of love and duty,
  As our being's end.

Earnest toil and strong endeavor
  Of a spirit which within
Wrestles with familiar evil
  And besetting sin;

And without, with tireless vigor,
  Steady heart, and weapon strong,
In the power of truth assailing
  Every form of wrong.

WORK.

What are we set on earth for? Say, to toil;
Nor seek to leave thy tending of the vines,
For all the heat o' the day, till it declines,
And Death's mild curfew shall from work assoil.
God did anoint thee with his odorous oil,
To wrestle, not to reign; and He assigns
All thy tears over, like pure crystallines,
For younger fellow-workers of the soil
To wear for amulets. So others shall
Take patience, labor, to their heart and hand,
From thy hand, and thy heart, and thy brave cheer,
And God's grace fructify through thee to all.
The least flower, with a brimming cup may stand,
And share its dew-drop with another near.

EMPLOYMENT.

If as a flower doth spread and die,
  Thou wouldst extend to me some good,
Before I were by frost's extremity
    Nipt in the bud,

The sweetness and the praise were thine,
  But the extension and the room,
Which in thy garland I should fill, were mine
    At thy great doom.

For as thou dost impart thy grace,
  The greater shall our glory be:
The measure of our joys is in this place,
    The stuff with thee.

Let me not languish then, and spend
  A life as barren to thy praise
As is the dust to which that life doth tend,
    But with delays.

Employment.

All things are busy; only I
Neither bring honey with the bees,
Nor flowers to make that, nor the husbandry
    To water these.

I am no link of thy great chain,
But all my company is a weed:
Lord, place me in thy concert, give one strain
    To my poor reed!

THE SAME DULL TASK AND WEARY WAY.

Day after day, until to-day,
   Imaged its fellows gone before;
The same dull task, the weary way,
   The weakness pardoned o'er and o'er;

The thwarted thirst, too faintly felt,
   For joy's wellnigh forgotten life;
The impatient heart, which, when I knelt,
   Made of my worship barren strife.

Ah, whence to-day's so sweet release?
   This clearance light of all my care;
This conscience free, this fertile peace,
   These softly folded wings of prayer;

This calm and more than conquering love,
   With which the tempter dares not cope;
This joy that lifts no glance above,
   For faith too sure, too sweet for hope?

Oh, happy time, too happy change,
　It will not live, though fondly nursed!
Sweet Day, which soon will seem as strange
　As now the Night which seems dispersed!

Adieu! But, while my heart is warmed,
　Some heavenly promise let me make:
Strong are those vows, and well performed,
　Which at such times we undertake.

IMPERFECTION OF HUMAN SYMPATHY

Why should we faint and fear to live alone,
    Since all alone — so Heaven has willed — we die,
Nor even the tenderest heart, and next our own,
    Knows half the reasons why we smile and sigh?

Each in his hidden sphere of joy or woe,
    Our hermit spirits dwell, and range apart;
Our eyes see all around, in gloom or glow,
    Hues of their own, fresh borrowed from the heart.

And well it is for us our God should feel
    Alone our secret throbbings: so our prayer
May readier spring to Heaven, nor spend its zeal
    On cloud-born idols of this lower air.

For if one heart in perfect sympathy
    Beat with another, answering love for love,
Weak mortals all entranced on earth would lie,
    Nor listen for those purer strains above.

Imperfection of Human Sympathy.

Or what if Heaven for once its searching light
  Lent to some partial eye, disclosing all
The rude, bad thoughts that in our bosom's night
  Wander at large, nor heed love's gentle thrall?

Who would not shun the dreary, uncouth place?
  As if, fond leaning where her infant slept,
A mother's arm a serpent should embrace:
  So might we friendless live, and die unwept.

Then keep the softening veil in mercy drawn,
  Thou who canst love us though thou read us true;
As on the bosom of the aerial lawn
  Melts in dim haze each coarse, ungentle hue.

Thou know'st our bitterness; our joys are thine;
  No stranger thou to all our wanderings wild:
Nor could we bear to think, how every line
  Of us, thy darkened likeness and defiled,

Stands in full sunshine of thy piercing eye,
  But that thou call'st us Brethren : sweet repose
Is in that word: the Lord who dwells on high
  Knows all, yet loves us better than he knows.

STRUGGLE NOT WITH THY LIFE.

STRUGGLE not with thy life! The heavy doom
   Resist not; it will bow thee like a slave:
Strive not! thou shalt not conquer; to thy tomb
   Thou shalt go crushed, and ground, though ne'er so brave.

Complain not of thy life! For what art thou
   More than thy fellows, that thou shouldst not weep?
Brave thoughts still lodge beneath a furrowed brow,
   And the way-wearied have the sweetest sleep.

Marvel not at thy life! Patience shall see
   The perfect work of wisdom to her given;
Hold fast thy soul through this high mystery,
   And it shall lead thee to the gates of heaven.

STILL HOPE! STILL ACT!

STILL hope! still act! Be sure that life,
   The source and strength of every good,
Wastes down in feeling's empty strife,
   And dies in dreaming's sickly mood.

To toil, in tasks however mean,
   For all we know of right and true, —
In this alone our worth is seen,
   'T is this we were ordained to do.

So shalt thou find in work and thought
   The peace that sorrow cannot give;
Though grief's worst pangs to thee be taught,
   By thee let others nobler live.

Oh, wail not in the darksome forest,
   Where thou must needs be left alone,
But, e'en when memory is sorest,
   Seek out a path, and journey on!

STRUGGLE NOT WITH THY LIFE.

Struggle not with thy life! The heavy doom
    Resist not; it will bow thee like a slave:
Strive not! thou shalt not conquer; to thy tomb
    Thou shalt go crushed, and ground, though ne'er so brave.

Complain not of thy life! For what art thou
    More than thy fellows, that thou shouldst not weep?
Brave thoughts still lodge beneath a furrowed brow,
    And the way-wearied have the sweetest sleep.

Marvel not at thy life! Patience shall see
    The perfect work of wisdom to her given;
Hold fast thy soul through this high mystery,
    And it shall lead thee to the gates of heaven.

STILL HOPE! STILL ACT!

Still hope! still act! Be sure that life,
　　The source and strength of every good,
Wastes down in feeling's empty strife,
　　And dies in dreaming's sickly mood.

To toil, in tasks however mean,
　　For all we know of right and true, —
In this alone our worth is seen,
　　'T is this we were ordained to do.

So shalt thou find in work and thought
　　The peace that sorrow cannot give;
Though grief's worst pangs to thee be taught,
　　By thee let others nobler live.

Oh, wail not in the darksome forest,
　　Where thou must needs be left alone,
But, e'en when memory is sorest,
　　Seek out a path, and journey on!

Still Hope! Still Act!

Thou wilt have angels near above,
  By whom invisible aid is given:
They journey still on tasks of love,
  And never rest, except in heaven.

Chi ha travaglio, in pace il porti!
Dolce è Dio, se il mondo è amaro;
Sappia l' uom che al cielo è caro;
Abbia fede, e avrà conforti.

HOPE FOR THE HOPELESS.

When, unveiled by Truth's compulsion,
   Life without a smile appears,
And the breaking heart's convulsion
   Finds no vent in words or tears,

Nought can cheer the dark existence
   Which we may not fly from yet;
But, with Fate's severe assistance,
   Though we live, we may forget.

Patience, quiet, toil, denial,
   These, though hard, are good for man;
And the martyred spirit's trial
   Gains it more than passion can.

This have thou and I been learning,
   Lessons strange to young and old;
But while loving, shrinking, yearning,
   Be it still the faith we hold.

For while woe is broad and patent,
    Filling, clouding all the sight,
Ever MELIORA LATENT,
    And a dawn will end the night.

MELIORA LATENT ever!
    Better than the seen lies hid;
Time the curtain's dusk will sever,
    And will raise the casket's lid.

This our hope for all that's mortal,
    And we too shall burst our bond;
Death keeps watch beside the portal,
    But 't is Life that dwells beyond.

Still the final hour befriends us,
    Nature's direst though it be;
And the fiercest pang that rends us
    Does its worst — and sets us free.

While our seekings, lingerings, fleeings,
    Most inflame us, most destroy,
It is much for weakest beings
    Still to hope, though not enjoy.

Then from earth's immediate sorrow
    Toward the skyey future turn,

And from its unseen to-morrow
Fill to-day's exhausted urn!

---

*Hope — with all the strength thou usest
  In embracing thy despair;
Love — the earthly love thou losest
  Shall return to thee more fair;
Work — make clear the forest-tangles
  Of the wildest stranger-land;
Trust — the blessed deathly angels
  Whisper " Sabbath hours at hand!"*

TU NE QUÆSIERIS!

ONLY the present is thy part and fee:
    And happy thou,
If, though thou didst not beat thy future brow,
    Thou couldst well see
  What present things required of thee.

God chains the dog till night: wilt loose the chain,
    And wake thy sorrow?
Wilt thou forestall it, and now grieve to-morrow,
    And then again
  Grieve over freshly all thy pain?

Either grief will not come, or if it must,
    Do not forecast:
And while it cometh, it is almost past.
    Away distrust!
  My God hath promised: he is just.

ANTICIPATION.

How beautiful the earth is still
   To thee,—how full of happiness!
How little fraught with real ill,
   Or unreal phantoms of distress!
How spring can bring thee glory, yet,
And summer win thee to forget
   December's sullen time!
Why dost thou hold the treasure fast
Of youth's delight, when youth is past,
   And thou art near thy prime?—
When those who were thy own compeers,
Equals in fortune and in years,
Have seen their morning melt in tears,
   To clouded, smileless day:
Blest, had they died untried and young,
Before their hearts went wandering wrong,
Poor slaves, subdued by passions strong,
   A weak and helpless prey!

" Because, I hoped while they enjoyed,
And, by fulfilment, hope destroyed:

Anticipation.

As children hope, with trustful breast,
I waited bliss, and cherished rest.
A thoughtful spirit taught me, soon,
That we must long till life be done;
That every phase of earthly joy
Must always fade, and always cloy.

"This I foresaw, and would not chase
   The fleeting treacheries;
But, with firm foot and tranquil face,
Held backward from that tempting race,
Gazed o'er the sands the waves efface,
   To the enduring seas:
There cast my anchor of desire,
   Deep in unknown eternity,
Nor ever let my spirit tire,
   With looking for what is to be.

"It is hope's spell that glorifies,
Like youth, to my maturer eyes,
All Nature's million mysteries,
   The fearful and the fair;
Hope soothes me in the griefs I know,
She lulls my pain for others' woe,
And makes me strong to undergo
   What I am born to bear.

"Glad comforter! will I not brave,
Unawed, the darkness of the grave,—

Nay, smile to hear Death's billows rave,
  Sustained, my guide, by thee?
The more unjust seems present fate,
The more my spirit swells elate,
Strong, in thy strength, to anticipate
  Rewarding destiny!"

ONWARD INTO LIGHT.

OUR course is onward, onward into light :
What though the darkness gathereth amain ?
Yet to return or tarry both are vain.
How tarry, when around us is thick night ?
Whither return ? what flower yet ever might,
In days of gloom and cold and stormy rain,
Inclose itself in its green bud again,
Hiding from wrath of tempest out of sight ?
Courage ! we travel through a darksome cave,
But still, as nearer to the light we draw,
Fresh gales will reach us from the upper air,
And wholesome dews of heaven our foreheads
      lave ;
The darkness lighten more, till, full of awe,
We stand in the open sunshine — unaware.

CARPE DIEM!

We live not in our moments or our years:
The present we fling from us like the rind
Of some sweet future, which we after find
Bitter to taste, or bind *that* in with fears,
And water it beforehand with our tears, —
　Vain tears for that which never may arrive :
　Meanwhile the joy whereby we ought to live,
Neglected, or unheeded, disappears.
Wiser it were to welcome and make ours
　Whate'er of good, though small, the present brings, —
Kind greetings, sunshine, song of birds, and flowers,
　With a child's pure delight in little things ;
And of the griefs unborn to rest secure,
Knowing that mercy ever will endure.

AGAINST DESPONDENCY.

Despair not in the vale of woe,
Where many joys from suffering flow.

Oft breathes simoom, and close behind
A breath of God doth softly blow.

Clouds threaten — but a ray of light,
And not of lightning, falls below.

How many winters o'er thy head
Have past, — yet bald it does not show.

Thy branches are not bare, — and yet
What storms have shook them to and fro.

To thee has time brought many joys,
If many it has bid to go;

And seasoned has with bitterness
Thy cup, that flat it should not grow.

Against Despondency.

Trust in that veilèd hand, which leads
None by the path that he would go;

And always be for change prepared,
For the world's law is ebb and flow.

Stand fast in suffering, until He
Who called it, shall dismiss also;

And from the Lord all good expect,
Who many mercies strews below, —

Who in life's narrow garden-strip
Has bid delights unnumbered blow.

AGAINST FOREBODING.

O THOU of dark forebodings drear,
O thou of such a faithless heart,
Hast thou forgotten what thou art,
That thou hast ventured so to fear?

No weed on Ocean's bosom cast,
Borne by its never-resting foam
This way and that, without an home,
Till flung on some bleak shore at last, —

But thou the Lotus, which, above,
Swayed here and there by wind and tide,
Yet still below doth fixed abide,
Fast rooted in eternal Love.

VAIN HOPES AND FEARS.

One time I was allowed to steer
　Through realms of azure light;
Henceforth, I said, I need not fear
　A lower, meaner flight;
But here shall evermore abide,
In light and splendor glorified.

My heart one time the rivers fed,
　Large dews upon it lay;
A freshness it has won, I said,
　Which shall not pass away,
But what it is, it shall remain,
Its freshness to the end retain.

But when I lay upon the shore,
　Like some poor wounded thing,
I deemed I should not ever more
　Refit my shattered wing,—
Nailed to the ground and fastened there:
This was the thought of my despair.

And when my very heart seemed dried,
    And parched as summer dust,
Such still I deemed it must abide;
    No hope had I, no trust
That any power again could bless
With fountains that waste wilderness.

But if both hope and fear were vain,
    And came alike to nought,
Two lessons we from this may gain,
    If aught can teach us aught, —
One lesson rather, — to divide
Between our fearfulness and pride.

THEY SERVE WHO STAND AND WAIT.

When I consider how my light is spent,
   Ere half my days, in this dark world and wide,
   And that one talent, which is death to hide,
Lodg'd with me useless, though my soul more bent
To serve therewith my Maker, and present
   My true account, lest he returning chide, —
   Doth God exact day-labor, light denied?
I fondly ask. But patience, to prevent
That murmur, soon replies, — God doth not need
   Either man's work, or his own gifts: who best
   Bear his mild yoke, they serve him best: his state
Is kingly; thousands at his bidding speed,
   And post o'er land and ocean without rest:
   They also serve who only stand and wait.

FOR GOD'S SAKE.

Teach me, my God and King,
  In all things Thee to see;
And what I do in anything,
  To do it as for Thee:

Not rudely, as a beast,
  To run into an action;
But still to make thee prepossest,
  And give it his perfection.

A man that looks on glass,
  On it may stay his eye;
Or, if he pleaseth, through it pass,
  And then the heaven espy.

All may of thee partake:
  Nothing can be so mean,
Which, with this tincture,—for Thy sake,
  Will not grow bright and clean.

For God's Sake.

A servant, with this clause,
    Makes drudgery divine :
Who sweeps a room, as for thy laws,
    Makes that, and the action, fine.

This is the famous stone
    That turneth all to gold ;
For that which God doth touch and own
    Cannot for less be told.

THOU CAM'ST NOT TO THY PLACE BY ACCIDENT.

Thou cam'st not to thy place by accident:
   It is the very place God meant for thee;
   And shouldst thou there small scope for action
      see,
Do not for this give room to discontent;
Nor let the time thou owest to God be spent
   In idly dreaming how thou mightest be,
   In what concerns thy spiritual life, more free
From outward hindrance or impediment:
For presently this hindrance thou shalt find
   That without which all goodness were a task
   So slight, that Virtue never could grow strong:
And wouldst thou do one duty to His mind,
   The Imposer's, — overburdened, thou shalt ask,
   And own thy need of grace to help, ere long.

ADEQUACY.

WE cannot say the morning sun fulfils
   Ingloriously its course ; nor that the clear
   Strong stars, without significance, insphere
Our habitation. We, meantime, our ills
Heap up against this good, and lift a cry
   Against this work-day world, this ill-spread feast,
As if ourselves were better certainly
   Than what we come to. Maker and High-Priest,
I ask thee not my joys to multiply, —
   Only to make me worthier of the least !

MY TIMES ARE IN THY HAND.

Father, I know that all my life
   Is portioned out for me,
And the changes that will surely come
   I do not fear to see;
But I ask thee for a present mind
   Intent on pleasing thee.

I ask thee for a thoughtful love,
   Through constant watching wise,
To meet the glad with joyful smiles,
   And to wipe the weeping eyes;
And a heart at leisure from itself
   To soothe and sympathize.

I would not have the restless will
   That hurries to and fro,
Seeking for some great thing to do,
   Or secret thing to know;
I would be treated as a child,
   And guided where I go.

Wherever in the world I am,
 In whatsoe'er estate,
I have a fellowship with hearts
 To keep and cultivate ;
And a work of lowly love to do
 For the Lord on whom I wait.

So I ask thee for the daily strength,
 To none that ask denied,
And a mind to blend with outward life,
 While keeping at thy side ;
Content to fill a little space,
 If Thou be glorified.

And if some things I do not ask
 In my cup of blessing be,
I would have my spirit filled the more
 With grateful love to thee ;
And careful less to serve thee much,
 Than to please thee perfectly.

There are briers besetting every path,
 Which call for patient care ;
There is a cross in every lot,
 And a need for earnest prayer ;
But a lowly heart that leans on thee
 Is happy anywhere.

In a service which thy love appoints
  There are no bonds for me;
For my secret heart is taught the truth
  That makes thy children free;
And a life of self-renouncing love
  Is a life of liberty.

THE BETTER PART.

TO A VIRTUOUS YOUNG LADY.

Lady, that in the prime of earliest youth
  Wisely hast shunn'd the broad way and the green,
And with those few art eminently seen
That labor up the hill of heavenly Truth,
The better part, with Mary and with Ruth,
  Chosen thou hast; and they that overween,
  And at thy growing virtues fret their spleen,
No anger find in thee, but pity and ruth.
Thy care is fixt, and zealously attends,
  To fill thy odorous lamp with deeds of light,
  And hope that reaps not shame. Therefore be sure
Thou, when the Bridegroom with his feastful friends
  Passes to bliss at the mid hour of night,
  Hast gain'd thy entrance, virgin wise and pure.

FAME.

What shall I do lest life in silence pass?
 And if it do,
And never prompt the bray of noisy brass,
 What need'st thou rue?
Remember, aye the ocean deeps are mute,
 The shallows roar:
Worth is the ocean; Fame is but the bruit
 Along the shore.

What shall I do to be forever known?
 Thy duty ever.
This did full many who yet slept unknown.
 Oh, never, never!
Think'st thou, perchance, that they remain unknown
 Whom *thou* know'st not?
By angel-trumps in heaven their praise is blown, —
 Divine their lot.

Fame.

What shall I do to gain eternal life?
    Discharge aright
The simple dues with which each day is rife?
    Yea, with thy might.
Ere perfect scheme of action thou devise,
    Will life be shed;
While he who ever acts as conscience cries
    Shall live, though dead.

TRUTH.

Fly from the world and dwell with Truthfulness;
Sufficient be thy wealth, albeit small;
Avarice hath hate, ambition carefulness,
And praise despite, yet good is mixed with all:
Taste no more sweets than to thy share may fall;
Counsel thyself, that well canst counsel give,
And fear not Truth shall teach thee how to live.

All that is sent thee take with cheerfulness, —
The wrestling of this world requires a fall,
Here is no home, here is but wilderness;
Pilgrim, advance! Poor beast, desert thy stall;
Look up on high, and thank thy God for all!
Forsake thy lusts, and with thy spirit strive,
And fear not Truth shall save thy soul alive!

DUTY.

* Stern Daughter of the Voice of God,
O Duty, if that name thou love,
Who art a light to guide, a rod
To check the erring, and reprove;
Thou, who art victory and law
When empty terrors overawe,
From vain temptations dost set free,
And calm'st the weary strife of frail humanity!

There are who ask not if thine eye
Be on them; who, in love and truth,
Where no misgiving is, rely
Upon the genial sense of youth:
Glad hearts, without reproach or blot,
Who do thy work, and know it not:
Oh! if, through confidence misplaced,
They fail, thy saving arms, dread Power, around
them cast!

Serene will be our days and bright,
And happy will our nature be,

When love is an unerring light,
  And joy its own security.
And they a blissful course may hold
Even now, who, not unwisely bold,
Live in the spirit of this creed,
Yet seek thy firm support, according to their
    need.

I, loving freedom, and untried,
  No sport of every random gust,
Yet being to myself a guide,
  Too blindly have reposed my trust:
And oft, when in my heart was heard
Thy timely mandate, I deferred
The task, in smoother walks to stray;
But thee I now would serve more strictly, if I
    may.

Through no disturbance of my soul,
  Or strong compunction in me wrought,
I supplicate for thy control;
  But in the quietness of thought.
Me this unchartered freedom tires;
I feel the weight of chance-desires;
My hopes no more must change their name;
I long for a repose that ever is the same.

Stern Lawgiver! yet thou dost wear
  The Godhead's most benignant grace;

Duty.

Nor know we anything so fair
  As is the smile upon thy face:
Flowers laugh before thee on their beds,
And fragrance in thy footing treads;
Thou dost preserve the stars from wrong;
And the most ancient heavens, through thee,
  are fresh and strong.

To humbler functions, awful Power!
  I call thee: I myself commend
Unto thy guidance from this hour;
  O let my weakness have an end!
Give unto me, made lowly wise,
The spirit of self-sacrifice;
The confidence of reason give;
And in the light of truth thy bondman let me
  live!

PEACE.

I have found Peace in the bright earth,
   And in the sunny sky;
By the low voice of summer seas,
   And where streams murmur by.

I find it in the quiet tone
   Of voices that I love;
By the flickering of a twilight fire,
   And in a leafless grove.

I find it in the silent flow
   Of solitary thought;
In calm, half-meditated dreams,
   And reasonings self-taught.

But seldom have I found such peace,
   As in the soul's deep joy
Of passing onward free from harm
   Through every day's employ.

THE CLOISTER.

THOUGHT never knew material bound or place,
Nor footsteps may the roving fancy trace:
Peace cannot learn beneath a roof to house,
Nor cloister hold us safe within our vows.

The cloistered heart may brave the common air,
And the world's children breathe the holiest
   prayer:
Build for us, Lord, and in thy temple reign!
Watch with us, Lord, our watchman wakes in
   vain!

THE WORTH OF HOURS.

BELIEVE not that your inner eye
Can ever in just measure try
The worth of hours as they go by.

For every man's weak self, alas!
Makes him to see them, while they pass,
As through a dim or tinted glass:

But if in earnest care you would
Mete out to each its part of good,
Trust rather to your after-mood.

Those surely are not fairly spent,
That leave your spirit bowed and bent
In sad unrest and ill-content:

And more, — though free from seeming harm,
You rest from toil of mind or arm,
Or slow retire from Pleasure's charm, —

If then a painful sense comes on
Of something wholly lost and gone,
Vainly enjoyed, or vainly done, —

Of something from your being's chain
Broke off, nor to be linked again
By all mere Memory can retain, —

Upon your heart this truth may rise, —
Nothing that altogether dies
Suffices man's just destinies.

So should we live, that every hour
May die as dies the natural flower, —
A self-reviving thing of power;

That every thought and every deed
May hold within itself the seed
Of future good and future meed;

Esteeming sorrow, whose employ
Is to develop, not destroy.
Far better than a barren joy.

THE INGRATITUDE OF THE HAPPY.

Some murmur when their sky is clear,
   And wholly bright to view,
If one small speck of dark appear
   In their great heaven of blue.
And some with thankful love are filled,
   If but one streak of light,
One ray of God's good mercy, gild
   The darkness of their night.

In palaces are hearts that ask,
   In discontent and pride,
Why life is such a dreary task,
   And all good things denied.
And hearts in poorest huts admire
   How love has in their aid
(Love that not ever seems to tire)
   Such rich provision made!

WERE THIS WORLD ONLY MADE FOR ME!

Unthinking, idle, wild, and young,
I laughed, and danced, and talked, and sung;
And, proud of health, of freedom vain,
Dreamed not of sorrow, care, or pain;
Concluding, in those hours of glee,
That all the world was made for me.

But when the hour of trial came,
When sickness shook this trembling frame,
When folly's gay pursuits were o'er,
And I could sing and dance no more,
It then occurred, how sad 't would be
Were this world only made for me.

LOVE'S SELF-REPROACH.

This did not once so trouble me,
That better I could not love Thee;
    But now I feel and know
That only when we love, we find
How far our hearts remain behind
    The love they should bestow.

While we had little care to call
On thee, and scarcely prayed at all,
    We seemed enough to pray:
But now we only think with shame
How seldom to thy glorious name
    Our lips their offerings pay.

And when we gave yet slighter heed
Unto our brother's suffering need,
    Our hearts reproached us then
Not half so much as now, that we
With such a careless eye can see
    The woes and wants of men.

Love's Self-Reproach.

In doing is this knowledge ours, —
To see what yet remains undone ;
 With this our pride repress,
And give us grace, a growing store,
That day by day we may do more,
 And may esteem it less!

CAST THY BREAD ON THE WATERS.

Oh be not faithless! with the morn,
   Scatter abroad thy grain ;
At noontide, — faint not thou forlorn ;
   At evening, — sow again !
Blessed are they, whate'er betide,
Who thus all waters sow beside.

Thou knowest not which seed shall grow,
   Or which may die or live ;
In faith and hope and patience, sow !
   The increase God shall give, —
According to his gracious will,
As best his purpose may fulfil.

EXAMPLE.

We scatter seeds with careless hand,
  And dream we ne'er shall see them more:
    But for a thousand years
    Their fruit appears,
In weeds, that mar the land,
  Or healthful store.

The deeds we do, the words we say, —
  Into still air they seem to fleet,
    We count them ever past;
    But they shall last, —
In the dread judgment they
  And we shall meet!

I charge thee by the years gone by,
  For the love's sake of brethren dear,
    Keep thou the one true way,
    In work and play,
Lest in that world their cry
  Of woe thou hear.

ABSENCE.

What shall I do with all the days and hours
    That must be counted ere I see thy face?
How shall I charm the interval that lowers
    Between this time and that sweet time of
        grace?

Shall I in slumber steep each weary sense,
    Weary with longing? Shall I flee away
Into past days, and with some fond pretence
    Cheat myself to forget the present day?

Shall love for thee lay on my soul the sin
    Of casting from me God's great gift of time?
Shall I these mists of memory lock'd within,
    Leave, and forget life's purposes sublime?

Oh how, or by what means, may I contrive
    To bring the hour that brings thee back more
        near?
How may I teach my drooping hope to live,
    Until that blessed time, and thou, art here?

Absence.

I 'll tell thee : for thy sake, I will lay hold
   Of all good aims, and consecrate to thee,
In worthy deeds, each moment that is told
   While thou, beloved one ! art far from me.

For thee, I will arouse my thoughts to try
   All heavenward flights, all high and holy strains ;
For thy dear sake, I will walk patiently
   Through these long hours, nor call their minutes pains.

I will this dreary blank of absence make
   A noble task-time, and will therein strive
To follow excellence, and to o'ertake
   More good than I have won since yet I live.

So may this doomèd time build up in me
   A thousand graces which shall thus be thine ;
So may my love and longing hallowed be,
   And thy dear thought an influence divine.

DISAPPOINTED AFFECTION.

If fate Love's dear ambition mar,
   And load his breast with hopeless pain,
And seem to blot out sun and star,
   Love, lost or won, is countless gain.
His sorrow boasts a secret bliss
   Which sorrow of itself beguiles,
And Love in tears too noble is
   For pity, save of Love in smiles.
But looking backward through his tears,
   With vision of maturer scope,
How often one dead joy appears
   The platform of some better hope!
And, let us own, the sharpest smart
   Which human patience may endure
Pays light for that which leaves the heart
   More generous, dignified, and pure.

Learn, by a mortal yearning to ascend, —
Seeking a higher object. Love was given,

*Encouraged, sanctioned, chiefly for that end ;
For this the passion to excess was driven, —
That self might be annulled ; her bondage prove
The fetters of a dream opposed to Love!*

A VALEDICTION.

God be with thee, my beloved, — God be with
 thee!
 Else alone thou goest forth,
 Thy face unto the north,
Moor and pleasance, all around thee and beneath
 thee,
 Looking equal in one snow:
 While I, who try to reach thee,
 Vainly follow, vainly follow,
 With the farewell and the hollo,
 And cannot reach thee so.
 Alas! I can but teach thee:
God be with thee, my beloved, — God be with
 thee!

Can I teach thee, my beloved, — can I teach
 thee?
 If I said, Go left or right,
 The counsel would be light,

A Valediction.

The wisdom poor of all that could enrich thee.
    My right would show like left;
    My raising would depress thee;
    My choice of light would blind thee;
    Of way, would leave behind thee;
    Of end, would leave bereft.
    Alas! I can but bless thee:
May God teach thee, my beloved, — may God
    teach thee!

Can I bless thee, my beloved, — can I bless thee?
    What blessing word can I
    From mine own tears keep dry?
What flowers grow in my field wherewith to dress
    thee?
    My good reverts to ill;
    My calmnesses would move thee;
    My softnesses would prick thee;
    My bindings-up would break thee;
    My crownings curse and kill.
    Alas! I can but love thee:
May God bless thee, my beloved, — may God
    bless thee!

Can I love thee, my beloved, — can I love thee?
    And is this like love, to stand
    With no help in my hand,

A Valediction.

When strong as death I fain would watch above
    thee?
  My love-kiss can deny
  No tear that falls beneath it;
  Mine oath of love can swear thee
  From no ill that comes near thee;
  And thou diest while I breathe it,
  And I — I can but die!
May God love thee, my beloved, — may God
    love thee!

FRIENDS PARTED BY OPINION.

As ships, becalmed at eve, that lay
   With canvas drooping, side by side,
Two towers of sail at dawn of day,
   Are scarce, long leagues apart, descried;

When fell the night, upsprung the breeze,
   And all the darkling hours they plied,
Nor dreamt but each the self-same seas
   By each was cleaving, side by side:

E'en so — but why the tale reveal
   Of those whom, year by year unchanged,
Brief absence joined anew to feel,
   Astounded, soul from soul estranged?

At dead of night their sails were filled,
   And onward each rejoicing steered:
Ah, neither blame, for neither willed,
   Or wist, what first with dawn appeared!

To veer, how vain! On, onward strain,
 Brave barks! In light, in darkness too,
Through winds and tides one compass guides;
 To that, and your own selves, be true.

But O blithe breeze, and O great seas,
 Though ne'er, that earliest parting past,
On your wide plain they join again,
 Together lead them home at last!

One port, methought, alike they sought,
 One purpose hold where'er they fare;
O bounding breeze, O rushing seas,
 At last, at last, unite them there!

THE MINISTRY OF LOVE.

I WOULD I were an excellent divine,
    That had the Bible at my fingers' ends,
That men might hear out of this mouth of mine
    How God doth make his enemies his friends,
Rather than with a thundering and long prayer
Be led into presumption or despair.

This would I be, and would none other be
    But a religious servant of my God;
To know there is none other God but He,
    And willingly to suffer Mercy's rod,
Joy in his grace, and live but in his love,
And seek my bliss but in the world above.

And I would frame a kind of faithful prayer
    For all estates within the state of grace,
That careful love might never know despair,
    Nor servile fear might faithful love deface;
And this would I both day and night devise
To make my humble spirit's exercise.

And I would read the rules of sacred life,
    Persuade the troubled soul to patience,
The husband care, and comfort to the wife,
    To child and servant due obedience,
Faith to the friend, and to the neighbor peace,
That love might live, and quarrels all might cease:

Pray for the health of all that are diseased,
    Confession unto all that are convicted,
And patience unto all that are displeased,
    And comfort unto all that are afflicted,
And mercy unto all that have offended,
And grace to all, that all may be amended!

THE KINGDOM OF GOD.

I say to thee, do thou repeat
To the first man thou mayest meet,
In lane, highway, or open street, —

That he, and we, and all men, move
Under a canopy of Love,
As broad as the blue sky above:

That doubt and trouble, fear and pain,
And anguish, all are shadows vain;
That death itself shall not remain:

That weary deserts we may tread,
A dreary labyrinth may thread,
Through dark ways underground be led:

Yet, if we will our Guide obey,
The dreariest path, the darkest way,
Shall issue out in heavenly day.

And we, on divers shores now cast,
Shall meet, our perilous voyage past,
All in our Father's home at last.

And ere thou leave him, say thou this,
Yet one word more: They only miss
The winning of that final bliss,

Who will not count it true that love, —
Blessing, not cursing, — rules above,
And that in it we live and move.

And one thing further make him know, —
That to believe these things are so,
This firm faith never to forego,

Despite of all which seems at strife
With blessing, all with curses rife, —
That this *is* blessing, this *is* life.

MY PSALM.

I MOURN no more my vanished years:
    Beneath a tender rain,
An April rain of smiles and tears,
    My heart is young again.

The west winds blow, and, singing low,
    I hear the glad streams run;
The windows of my soul I throw
    Wide open to the sun.

No longer forward nor behind
    I look in hope or fear;
But, grateful, take the good I find,
    The best of now and here.

I plough no more a desert land,
    To harvest weed and tare;
The manna dropping from God's hand
    Rebukes my painful care.

My Psalm.

I break my pilgrim staff, I lay
    Aside the toiling oar;
The angel sought so far away
    I welcome at my door.

All as God wills, who wisely heeds
    To give or to withhold,
And knoweth more of all my needs
    Than all my prayers have told!

Enough that blessings undeserved
    Have marked my erring track;
That wheresoe'er my feet have swerved,
    His chastening turned me back;

That more and more a Providence
    Of Love is understood,
Making the springs of time and sense
    Sweet with eternal good;

That death seems but a covered way
    Which opens into light,
Wherein no blinded child can stray
    Beyond the Father's sight;

That care and trial seem at last,
    Through Memory's sunset air,

Like mountain-ranges overpast,
  In purple distance fair.

And so the shadows fall apart,
  And so the west winds play;
And all the windows of my heart
  I open to the day.

ANDREW RYKMAN'S PRAYER.

ANDREW RYKMAN 's dead and gone:
   You can see his leaning slate
In the graveyard, and thereon
   Read his name and date.

"*Trust is truer than our fears,*"
   Runs the legend through the moss,
"*Gain is not in added years,*
   Nor in death is loss."

Still the feet that thither trod,
   All the friendly eyes are dim;
Only Nature, now, and God
   Have a care for him.

There the dews of quiet fall,
   Singing birds and soft winds stray:
Shall the tender Heart of All
   Be less kind than they?

What he was and what he is
  They who ask may haply find,
If they read this prayer of his
  Which he left behind.

Pardon, Lord, the lips that dare
Shape in words a mortal's prayer!
Prayer, that, when my day is done,
And I see its setting sun,
Shorn and beamless, cold and dim,
Sink beneath the horizon's rim, —
When this ball of rock and clay
Crumbles from my feet away,
And the solid shores of sense
Melt into the vague immense,
Father! I may come to thee
Even with the beggar's plea,
As the poorest of thy poor,
With my needs, and nothing more.

Not as one who seeks his home,
With a step assured, I come;
Still behind the tread I hear
Of my life-companion, Fear;
Still a shadow deep and vast
From my westering feet is cast,

Wavering, doubtful, undefined,
Never shapen nor outlined:
From myself the fear has grown,
And the shadow is my own.
Well I know that all things move
To the spheral rhythm of love, —
That to thee, O Lord of all!
Nothing can of chance befall:
Child and seraph, mote and star,
Well thou knowest what we are;
Through thy vast creative plan
Looking, from the worm to man,
There is pity in thine eyes,
But no hatred nor surprise.
Not in blind caprice of will,
Not in cunning sleight of skill,
Not for show of power, was wrought
Nature's marvel in thy thought.
Never careless hand and vain
Smites these chords of joy and pain;
No immortal selfishness
Plays the game of curse and bless:
Heaven and earth are witnesses
That thy glory goodness is.
Not for sport of mind and force
Hast thou made thy universe,
But as atmosphere and zone
Of thy loving heart alone.

Man, who walketh in a show,
Sees before him, to and fro,
Shadow and illusion go ;
All things flow and fluctuate,
Now contract and now dilate.
In the welter of this sea,
Nothing stable is but Thee ;
In this whirl of swooning trance,
Thou alone art permanence ;
All without thee only seems ;
All beside is choice of dreams.
Never yet in darkest mood
Doubted I that thou wast good,
Nor mistook my will for fate,
Pain of sin for heavenly hate ;
Never dreamed the gates of pearl
Rise from out the burning marl,
Or that good can only live
Of the bad conservative,
And through counterpoise of hell
Heaven alone be possible.

For myself alone I doubt ;
All is well, I know, without ;
I alone the beauty mar,
I alone the music jar.
Yet, with hands by evil stained,
And an ear by discord pained,

I am groping for the keys
Of the heavenly harmonies;
Still within my heart I bear
Love for all things good and fair.
Hand of want or soul in pain
Has not sought my door in vain;
I have kept my fealty good
To the human brotherhood;
Scarcely have I asked in prayer
That which others might not share.
I, who hear with secret shame
Praise that paineth more than blame,
Rich alone in favors lent,
Virtuous by accident,
Doubtful where I fain would rest,
Frailest where I seem the best,
Only strong for lack of test, —
What am I, that I should press
Special pleas of selfishness,
Coolly mounting into heaven
On my neighbor unforgiven?
Ne'er to me, howe'er disguised,
Comes a saint unrecognized;
Never fails my heart to greet
Noble deed with warmer beat;
Halt and maimed, I own not less
All the grace of holiness;
Nor, through shame or self-distrust,

Less I love the pure and just.
Thou, O Elder Brother! who
In thy flesh our trial knew,
Thou, who hast been touched by these
Our most sad infirmities,
Thou alone the gulf canst span
In the dual heart of man,
And between the soul and sense
Reconcile all difference;
Change the dream of me and mine
For the truth of thee and thine,
And, through chaos, doubt, and strife,
Interfuse thy calm of life.

Haply, thus by Thee renewed,
In thy borrowed goodness good,
Some sweet morning yet in God's
Dim, æonian periods,
Joyful I shall wake to see
Those I love who rest in thee,
And to them in thee allied
Shall my soul be satisfied.
Scarcely Hope hath shaped for me
What the future life may be.
Other lips may well be bold;
Like the publican of old,
I can only urge the plea,
" Lord, be merciful to me!"

Nothing of desert I claim,
Unto me belongeth shame.
Not for me the crowns of gold,
Palms, and harpings manifold;
Not for erring eye and feet
Jasper wall and golden street.
What thou wilt, O Father, give!
All is gain that I receive.
If my voice I may not raise
In the elders' song of praise,
If I may not, sin-defiled,
Claim my birthright as a child,
Suffer it that I to thee
As an hired servant be;
Let the lowliest task be mine,
Grateful, so the work be thine;
Let me find the humblest place
In the shadow of thy grace:
Blest to me were any spot
Where temptation whispers not.
If there be some weaker one,
Give me strength to help him on;
If a blinder soul there be,
Grant that I his guide may be.
Make my mortal dreams come true
With the work I fain would do;
Clothe with life the weak intent,
Let me be the thing I meant;

Let me find in thy employ
Peace that dearer is than joy;
Out of self to love be led,
And to heaven acclimated,
Until all things sweet and good
Seem my natural habitude.

VENI, SANCTE SPIRITUS.

Veni, Sancte Spiritus,
Et emitte cœlitus
  Lucis tuæ radium:
Veni, pater pauperum,
Veni, dator munerum,
  Veni, lumen cordium!

Consolator optime,
Dulcis hospes animæ,
  Dulce refrigerium:
In labore requies,
In æstu temperies,
  In fletu solatium!

O lux beatissima,
Reple cordis intima
  Tuorum fidelium!
Sine tuo numine,
Nihil est in homine,
  Nihil est innoxium.

KING ROBERT'S HYMN.

Holy Spirit! Fire divine!
Send from heaven a ray of thine,
  Lighten our obscurity:
Come, thou Father of the poor;
Come, thou Giver and Renewer,—
  Fountain of all purity!

Visit us, Consoler best!
Thou the bosom's sweetest guest,
  Sweetest comfort proffering:
Thou dost give the weary rest,
Shade to all with heat opprest,
  Solace in all suffering.

O blest Light ineffable!
With thy faithful amply dwell:
  Lord of our humanity,
Nothing lives without thy ray;
Reft of thy enlivening day,
  All is void and vanity.

Veni, Sancte Spiritus.

Lava quod est sordidum,
Riga quod est aridum,
   Sana quod est saucium,
Flecte quod est rigidum,
Fove quod est frigidum,
   Rege quod est devium!

Da tuis fidelibus,
In te confidentibus,
   Sacrum septenarium:
Da virtutis meritum,
Da salutis exitum,
   Da perenne gaudium!

King Robert's Hymn.

What is foul, oh! purify,
Water what in us is dry,
   All our hurts alleviate,
Bend our temper's rigidness,
Warm our nature's frigidness,
   Bring back all who deviate!

Give them who in thee abide,
All that do in thee confide,
   Give them grace increasingly:
Give to virtue its reward,
Saving end to all accord,
   Joy in heaven unceasingly!

FOR INSPIRATION.

BEN sarian dolci le preghiere mie,
   Se virtù mi prestassi da pregarte ;
   Nel mio terreno infertil non è parte
Da produr frutto di virtù natìe.

Tu il seme se' dell' opre giuste e pie,
   Che là germoglian dove ne fai parte ;
   Nessun proprio valor può seguitarte,
Se non gli mostri le tue belle vie.

Tu nella mente mia pensieri infondi
   Che producano in me sì vivi effetti,
   Signor, ch' io segua i tuoi vestigi santi ;

E dalla lingua mia chiari e facondi
   Sciogli della tua gloria ardenti detti,
   Perchè sempre io ti lodi, esalti, e canti.

FOR INSPIRATION.

The prayers I make will then be sweet indeed,
   If Thou the spirit give by which I pray:
   My unassisted heart is barren clay,
That of its native self can nothing feed:

Of good and pious works thou art the seed,
   That quickens only where thou sayst it may:
   Unless thou show to us thine own true way,
No man can find it; Father! thou must lead.

Do thou then breathe those thoughts into my mind,
   By which such virtue may in me be bred,
   That in thy holy footsteps I may tread;

The fetters of my tongue do thou unbind,
   That I may have the power to sing of thee,
   And sound thy praises everlastingly.

FOR INSPIRATION.

O LIVING will that shalt endure
   When all that seems shall suffer shock,
   Rise in the spiritual rock,
Flow through our deeds, and make them pure!

That we may lift from out the dust
   A voice as unto him that hears,
   A cry above the conquered years,
To one that with us works, and trust,

With faith that comes of self-control,
   The truths that never can be proved
   Until we close with all we loved,
And all we flow from, soul in soul.

SELF-DEVOTION AND RESIGNATION.

Come, Self-Devotion, high and pure,
Thoughts that in thankfulness endure,
Though dearest hopes are faithless found,
And dearest hearts are bursting round;
Come, Resignation, spirit meek,
And let me kiss thy placid cheek,
And read in thy pale eye serene
Their blessing, who by faith can wean
Their hearts from sense, and learn to love
God only, and the joys above.

They say, who know the life divine,
And upward gaze with eagle eyne,
That by each golden crown on high,
Rich with celestial jewelry,
Which for our Lord's redeemed is set,
There hangs a radiant coronet,
All gemmed with pure and living light,
Too dazzling for a sinner's sight,
Prepared for virgin souls, and them
Who seek the martyr's diadem.

Nor deem, who to that bliss aspire
Must win their way through blood and fire.
The writhings of a wounded heart
Are fiercer than a foeman's dart.
Oft in life's stillest shade reclining,
In desolation unrepining,
Without a hope on earth to find
A mirror in an answering mind,
Meek souls there are, who little dream
Their daily strife an angel's theme,
Or that the rod they take so calm,
Shall prove in heaven a martyr's palm.

And there are souls that seem to dwell
Above this earth, — so rich a spell
Floats round their steps, where'er they move,
From hopes fulfilled, and mutual love.
Such, if on high their thoughts are set,
Nor in the stream the source forget,
If prompt to quit the bliss they know,
Following the Lamb where'er he go,
By purest pleasures unbeguiled
To idolize or wife or child;
Such wedded souls our God shall own
For faultless virgins round his throne.

NEW CREATION.

Thou spakest: and the waters rolled
  Back from the Earth away;
They fled, by thy strong voice controlled,
  Till thou didst bid them stay:
Then did that rushing mighty ocean
Like a tame creature cease its motion,
Nor dared to pass where'er thy hand
Had fixed its bound of slender sand.

And freshly risen from out the deep
  The land lay tranquil now,
Like a new-christened child asleep,
  With the dew upon its brow:
As when in after-time the Earth
Rose from her second watery birth,
In pure baptismal garments drest,
And calmly waiting to be blest.

Again thou spakest, Lord of Power,
  And straight the land was seen

All clad with tree, and herb, and flower,
    A robe of lustrous green :
Like souls wherein the hidden strength
Of their new birth has waked at length,
When, robed in holiness, they tell
What might did in those waters dwell.

Lord, o'er the waters of my soul
    The word of power be said ;
Its thoughts and passions bid thou roll
    Each in its channelled bed ;
Till that in peaceful order flowing,
They time their glad, obedient going
To thy commands, whose voice to-day
Bade the tumultuous floods obey.

For restless as the moaning sea,
    The wild and wayward will
From side to side is wearily
    Changing and tossing still ;
But sway'd by thee, 't is like the river
That down its green banks flows forever,
And, calm and constant, tells to all
The blessedness of such sweet thrall.

Then in my heart, Spirit of Might,
    Awake the life within,

And bid a spring-tide, calm and bright,
　Of holiness begin :
So let it lie with Heaven's grace
Full shining on its quiet face,
Like the young Earth in peace profound,
Amid the assuagèd waters round.

FOR GRACE.

My stock lies dead, and no increase
   Doth my dull husbandry improve:
Oh let thy graces without cease
     Drop from above!

If still the sun should hide his face,
   Thy house would but a dungeon prove,
Thy works night's captives: oh let grace
     Drop from above!

The dew doth every morning fall:
   And shall the dew outstrip thy dove?
The dew for which grass cannot call
     Drop from above!

Death is still working like a mole,
   And digs my grave at each remove:
Let grace work too, and on my soul
     Drop from above!

For Grace.

Sin is still hammering my heart
　Unto a hardness void of love :
Let suppling grace, to cross his art,
　　Drop from above !

Oh come ! for thou dost know the way ;
　Or if to me thou wilt not move,
Remove me where I need not say
　　Drop from above !

FOR ENTIRE DEVOTION.

I pray not, Lord, to be redeemed from mortal
    sorrow;
  Redeem me only from my vain and mean
    self-love;
Then let each night of grief lead in a mourning
    morrow,
  Fear shall not shake my trust in thee, my
    peace above.

Yet while the Resurrection waves its signs au-
    gust,
  Like morning's dewy banners on a cloudless
    sky,
My weak feet cling enamored to the parching
    dust,
  And, on the sand, poor pebbles lure my roving
    eye.

Ye witnessings of silent, sad Gethsemane,
  That shaded garden whence light breaks for
    all our earth,

For Entire Devotion. 231

Around my anguish let your faithful influence be!
Ye prayers and sighs divine, be my immortal
  birth!

Vales of repentance mount to hills of high de-
  sire;
Seven times seven suffering years earn the
  Sabbatic rest;
Earth's fickle, cruel lap, — alternate frost and
  fire, —
Tempers beloved disciples for the Master's
  breast.

O Way for all that live! heal us by pain and loss;
Fill all our years with toil, and bless us with
  thy rod:
Thy bonds bring wider freedom; climbing, by
  the cross,
Wins that brave height where looms the city
  of our God!

O Sunshine. rising ever on our nights of sadness!
O best of all our good, and pardoner of our
  sin!
Look down with pity on our unbelieving mad-
  ness,
To Heaven's great welcome take us, homesick
  pilgrims, in!

For Entire Devotion.

Spirit that overcame the world's long tribulation,
  Try faltering faith, and make it firm through much enduring;
Feed weary hearts with patient hopes of thy salvation;
  Make strait submission, more than luxury's ease, alluring.

Hallow our wit with prayer; our mastery steep in meekness;
  Pour on our study inspiration's holy light;
Hew out for Christ's dear Church a future without weakness,
  Quarried from thine eternal Beauty, Order, Might!

Met, there, mankind's great brotherhood of souls and powers,
  Raise thou full praises from its farthest corners dim;
Pour down, O steadfast Sun, thy beams on all its towers;
  Roll through its world-wide spaces Faith's majestic hymn!

WATCH, PRAY, AND WORK!

CHEEK grow pale, but heart be vigorous!
   Body fall, but soul have peace!
Welcome, pain! thou searcher rigorous!
   Slay me, but my faith increase.

Sin, o'er sense so softly stealing,
   Doubt, that would my strength impair,
Hence at once from life and feeling!
   Now my cross I gladly bear.

Up, my soul! with clear sedateness
   Read Heaven's law, writ bright and broad;
Up! a sacrifice to greatness,
   Truth, and goodness, — up to God!

Up to labor! from thee shaking
   Off the bonds of sloth, be brave!
Give thyself to prayer and waking;
   Toil some fainting heart to save!

EIN' FESTE BURG IST UNSER GOTT.

Ein' feste Burg ist unser Gott,
   Ein' gute Wehr und Waffen;
Er hilft uns frei aus aller Noth
   Die uns jetzt hat betroffen.
Der alt' böse Feind,
Mit Ernst er's jetzt meint;
Gross' Macht und viel List
Sein' grausam Rüstung ist;
   Auf Erd' ist nicht sein's Gleichen.

Mit unsrer Macht ist nichts gethan,
   Wir sind gar bald verloren;
Es streit't für uns der rechte Mann,
   Den Gott selbst hat erkoren.
Fragst du, wer der ist?
Er heisst Jesus Christ,
Der Herr Zebaoth,
Und ist kein andrer Gott:
   Das Feld muss er behalten.

A MIGHTY FORTRESS IS OUR GOD.

A MIGHTY fortress is our God,
    A bulwark never failing;
Our helper he amid the flood
    Of mortal ills prevailing.
For still our ancient foe
Doth seek to work us woe;
His craft and power are great,
And, armed with cruel hate,
    On earth is not his equal.

Did we in our own strength confide,
    Our striving would be losing;
Were not the right man on our side,
    The man of God's own choosing.
Dost ask who that may be?
Christ Jesus, it is he.
Lord Sabaoth his name,
From age to age the same,
    And he must win the battle.

Und wenn die Welt voll Teufel wär',
   Und wollt'n uns gar verschlingen,
So fürchten wir uns nicht so sehr,
   Es soll uns doch gelingen.
Der Fürst dieser Welt,
Wie sauer er sich stellt,
Thut er uns doch nichts;
Das macht, er ist gericht't,
   Ein Wörtlein kann ihn fällen.

Das Wort sie sollen lassen stahn,
   Und kein'n Dank dazu haben;
Er ist bei uns wohl auf dem Plan,
   Mit seinem Geist und Gaben.
Nehmen sie den Leib,
Gut, Ehr', Kind und Weib;
Lass fahren dahin,
Sie haben's kein'n Gewinn;
   Das Reich muss uns doch bleiben.

A Mighty Fortress is our God.

And though this world, with devils filled,
　　Should threaten to undo us,
We will not fear, for God hath willed
　　His truth to triumph through us.
The Prince of Darkness grim,
We tremble not for him;
His rage we can endure,
For, lo! his doom is sure,
　　One little word shall fell him.

That word above all earthly powers —
　　No thanks to them — abideth;
The spirit and the gifts are ours
　　Through Him who with us sideth.
Let goods and kindred go,
This mortal life also;
The body they may kill,
God's truth abideth still,
　　His kingdom is forever.

MORGENLIED.

Seele, du musst munter werden,
  Denn der Erden
Blickt hervor ein neuer Tag;
Komm, dem Schöpfer dieser Strahlen
  Zu bezahlen,
Was dein schwacher Trieb vermag.

Deine Pflicht kannst du erlernen
  Von den Sternen,
Deren Gold der Sonne weicht;
So lass auch vor Gott zerrinnen,
  Was den Sinnen
Hier im Finstern schöne deucht.

Schau wie das was Athem ziehet
  Sich bemühet
Um der Sonnen holdes Licht;
Wie sich, was nur Wachsthum spüret,
  Freudig rühret,
Wenn ihr Glanz die Schatten bricht.

MORNING HYMN.

Come, my soul, thou must be waking;
Now is breaking
  O'er the earth another day;
Come, to Him who made this splendor,
See thou render
  All thy feeble powers can pay.

From the stars thy course be learning;
Dimly burning,
  Neath the sun their light grows pale:
So let all that sense delighted,
While benighted,
  From God's presence fade and fail.

Lo! how all of breath partaking,
Gladly waking,
  Hail the sun's enlivening light!
Plants, whose life mere sap doth nourish,
Rise and flourish,
  When he breaks the shades of night.

So lass dich auch fertig finden
Anzuzünden
Deinen Weihrauch, weil die Nacht,
Da dich Gott vor Unglücks-stürmen
Wollen schirmen,
Nun so glücklich hingebracht.

Bitte dass er dir Gedeihen
Mag verleihen,
Wenn du auf was gutes zielst;
Aber dass er dich mag stören,
Und bekehren,
Wenn du bose Regung fühlst.

Denk dass er auf deinen Wegen
Stets zugegen,
Dass er allen Sündenwust,
Ja die Schmach verborgner Flecken
Kann entdecken,
Und errathen was du thust.

Kränkt dich etwas diesen Morgen,
Lass Gott sorgen,
Der es wie die Sonne macht,
Welche pflegt der Berge Spitzen
Zu erhitzen,
Und auch in die Thäler lacht.

Morning Hymn.

Thou, too, hail the light returning,
Ready burning
   Be the incense of thy powers;
For the night is safely ended;
God hath tended
   With his care thy helpless hours.

Pray that he may prosper ever
Each endeavor,
   When thine aim is good and true;
But that he may ever thwart thee,
And convert thee,
   When thou evil wouldst pursue.

Think that he thy ways beholdeth;
He unfoldeth
   Every fault that lurks within;
Every stain of shame glossed over
Can discover,
   And discern each deed of sin.

If aught of care this morn oppress thee,
To him address thee,
   Who, like the sun, is good to all:
He gilds the mountain-tops, the while
His gracious smile
   Will on the humblest valley fall.

Um das was er dir verliehen
      Wird er ziehen
Eine Burg die Flammen streut:
Du wirst zwischen Legionen
      Engel wohnen,
Die der Satan selber scheut.

Morning Hymn.

Round the gifts his bounty showers,
Walls and towers
Girt with flames thy God shall rear:
Angel legions to defend thee
Shall attend thee,
Hosts whom Satan's self shall fear.

MORGENLIED.

Wenn ich einst von jenem Schlummer,
    Welcher Tod heisst, aufersteh',
Und von dieses Lebens Kummer
    Frei, den schönern Morgen seh',
O dann wach' ich anders auf;
Schon am Ziel ist dann mein Lauf;
Träume sind des Pilgers Sorgen,
Grosser Tag, an deinem Morgen.

Hilf dass keiner meiner Tage,
    Geber der Unsterblichkeit,
Jenem Richtenden einst sage,
    Er sei ganz von mir entweiht!
Auch noch heute wacht' ich auf,
Dank dir, Herr; zu dir hinauf
Führ' mich jeder meiner Tage,
Jede Freude, jede Plage.

Dass ich gern sie vor mir sehe,
    Wenn ihr letzter nun erscheint,

MORNING HYMN.

When I rise again to life
   From the tranquil sleep of death,
And, released from earthly strife,
   Breathe that morning's balmy breath,
I shall wake to other thought;
The race is run, the fight is fought;
All the pilgrim's cares are dreams,
When that dawn of morning gleams.

Help that no departed day,
   God of endless life and joy,
To the righteous Judge may say,
   'T was profaned by my employ.
To another morn I wake,
And to thee my offering make:
Oh may all my days that flee,
Joys and sorrows, lead to thee.

Gladly may I see them fled,
   When the twilight o'er me creeps,

Wenn zum dunkeln Thal' ich gehe,
  Und mein Freund nun um mich weint!
Lindre dann des Todes Pein,
Und lass mich den stärksten sein,
Mich, der ihn gen Himmel weise,
Und dich, Herr des Todes, preise!

When the darkening vale I tread,
  And my friend beside me weeps!
Death assuage, the pang remove,
Let me then the stronger prove,
Vanquishing with heavenward breath,
While I praise thee, Lord of death!

EVENING HYMN.

'T is gone, that bright and orbèd blaze,
Fast fading from our wistful gaze;
Yon mantling cloud has hid from sight
The last faint pulse of quivering light.

Sun of my soul, thou Saviour dear,
It is not night, if thou be near:
Oh may no earth-born cloud arise
To hide thee from thy servant's eyes!

When the soft dews of kindly sleep
My wearied eyelids gently steep,
Be my last thought, how sweet to rest
Forever on my Saviour's breast!

Abide with me from morn till eve,
For without thee I cannot live;
Abide with me when night is nigh,
For without thee I dare not die!

ABIDE WITH ME.

Abide with me! Fast falls the eventide;
The darkness thickens; Lord, with me abide:
When other helpers fail, and comforts flee,
Help of the helpless, oh abide with me!

Swift to its close ebbs out life's little day;
Earth's joys grow dim, its glories pass away:
Change and decay in all around I see;
O thou who changest not, abide with me!

Not a brief glance I beg, a passing word;
But as thou dwelt'st with thy disciples, Lord,
Familiar, condescending, patient, free,
Come, not to sojourn, but abide, with me.

Come, not in terrors, as the King of kings;
But kind and good, with healing in thy wings,
Tears for all woes, a heart for every plea;
Come, friend of sinners, and thus bide with me.

Abide with Me.

Thou on my head in early youth didst smile,
And, though rebellious and perverse meanwhile,
Thou hast not left me, oft as I left thee:
On to the close, O Lord, abide with me!

I need thy presence every passing hour:
What but thy grace can foil the Tempter's power?
Who like thyself my guide and stay can be?
Through cloud and sunshine, oh abide with me!

I fear no foe, with thee at hand to bless,
Ills have no weight, and tears no bitterness:
Where is death's sting? where, grave, thy victory?
I triumph still, if thou abide with me.

Hold thou thy cross before my closing eyes;
Shine through the gloom, and point me to the skies!
Heaven's morning breaks, and earth's vain shadows flee!
In life, in death, O Lord, abide with me.

EMMAUS.

Abide with us, O wondrous guest!
A stranger still, though long possessed;
Our hearts thy love unknown desire,
And marvel how the sacred fire
Should burn within us, while we stray
From that sad spot where Jesus lay.

So when our youth, through bitter loss,
Or hopes deferred, draws near the Cross,
We lose the Lord our childhood knew,
And God's own word may seem untrue:
Yet Christ himself shall soothe the way
Towards the evening of our day.

And though we travel towards the west,
'T is still for toil and not for rest;
No fate except with life is done;
At Emmaus is our work begun;
Then let us watch, lest tears should hide
The Lord who journeys by our side!

EVENING HYMN.

The night is come; like to the day
Depart not thou, great God, away:
Let not my sins, black as the night,
Eclipse the lustre of thy light.
Keep still in my horizon; for to me
The sun makes not the day, but thee.
Thou whose nature cannot sleep,
On my temples sentry keep;
Guard me 'gainst those watchful foes
Whose eyes are open while mine close.
Let no dreams my head infest,
But such as Jacob's temples blest;
While I do rest, my soul advance;
Make my sleep a holy trance;
That I may, my rest being wrought,
Awake into some holy thought;
And with active vigor run
My course, as doth the nimble sun.
Sleep is a death; oh make me try,
By sleeping, what it is to die;

Evening Hymn.

And as gently lay my head
On my grave, as now my bed.
Howe'er I rest, great God, let me
Awake again, at least with thee;
And thus assured, behold, I lie
Securely, or to wake or die.
These are my drowsy days; in vain
I do now wake, to sleep again:
Oh come that hour, when I shall never
Sleep again, but wake for ever!

SLEEP.

Of all the thoughts of God that are
Borne inward unto souls afar,
Along the Psalmist's music deep,
Now tell me if that any is,
For gift or grace, surpassing this, —
" He giveth his beloved, sleep ? "

What would we give to *our* beloved ?
The hero's heart, to be unmoved, —
The poet's star-tuned harp, to sweep, —
The patriot's voice, to teach and rouse, —
The monarch's crown, to light the brows ?
" He giveth his beloved, sleep."

What do we give to our beloved?
A little faith, all undisproved, —
A little dust, to overweep, —
And bitter memories, to make
The whole earth blasted for our sake.
" He giveth His beloved sleep."

Sleep.

Sleep soft, beloved! we sometimes say,
But have no tune to charm away
Sad dreams that through the eyelids creep:
But never doleful dream again
Shall break the happy slumber, when
" He giveth his beloved, sleep."

O earth, so full of dreary noises!
O men, with wailing in your voices!
O delved gold the wailers heap!
O strife, O curse, that o'er it fall!
God makes a silence through you all,
And "giveth his beloved, sleep."

His dews drop mutely on the hill,
His cloud above it saileth still,
Though on its slope men sow and reap:
More softly than the dew is shed,
Or cloud is floated overhead,
" He giveth his beloved, sleep."

For me, my heart, that erst did go
Most like a tired child at a show,
That sees through tears the jugglers leap,
Would now its wearied vision close,
Would childlike on his love repose
Who " giveth his beloved, sleep."

And friends, dear friends, when it shall be
That this low breath is gone from me,
And round my bier ye come to weep,
Let one, most loving of you all,
Say, "Not a tear must o'er her fall:
He giveth his beloved, sleep."

PRAISES FOR THIS WORLD.

PRAISÈD be the mosses soft
In thy forest pathways oft,
And the thorns, which make us think
Of the thornless river-brink,
   Where the ransomed tread!
Praisèd be thy sunny gleams,
And the storm, that worketh dreams
   Of calm unfinished!
Praisèd be thine active days,
And thy night-time's solemn need,
When in God's dear book we read
   No night shall be therein.
Praisèd be thy dwellings warm,
By household fagot's cheerful blaze,
Where, to hear of pardoned sin,
Pauseth oft the merry din,
Save the babe's upon the arm,
Who croweth to the crackling wood.
Yea, — and better understood,

Praisèd be thy dwellings cold,
Hid beneath the church-yard mould,
Where the bodies of the saints,
Separate from earthly taints,
Lie asleep, in blessing bound,
Waiting for the trumpet's sound
To free them into blessing ; — none
Weeping more beneath the sun.

FOREGLEAMS OF A HEAVENLY COUNTRY.

Morn, when before the sun his orb unshrouds,
    Swift as a beacon torch the light has sped,
Kindling the dusky summits of the clouds
    Each to a fiery red, —

The slanted columns of the noonday light,
    Let down into the bosom of the hills,
Or sunset, that with golden vapor bright
    The purple mountains fills, —

These made him say, — If God has so arrayed
    A fading world that quickly passes by, —
Such rich provision of delight has made
    For every human eye, —

What shall the eyes that wait for him survey,
    Where his own presence gloriously appears,
In worlds that were not founded for a day,
    But for eternal years!

And if at seasons this world's undelight
    Oppressed him, or the hollow at its heart,
One glance at those enduring mansions bright
    Made gloomier thoughts depart;

Till many times the sweetness of the thought
    Of an eternal country, where it lies
Removed from care and mortal anguish, brought
    Sweet tears into his eyes.

Thus, not unsolaced, he longwhile abode,
    Filling all dreary, melancholy time,
And empty spaces of the heart, with God,
    And with this hope sublime.

ON A BEAUTIFUL DAY.

O UNSEEN Spirit! now a calm divine
   Comes forth from thee, rejoicing earth and air!
Trees, hills, and houses, all distinctly shine,
   And thy great ocean slumbers everywhere.

The mountain ridge against the purple sky
   Stands clear and strong, with darkened rocks and dells,
And cloudless brightness opens wide on high
   A home aerial, where thy presence dwells.

The chime of bells remote, the murmuring sea,
   The song of birds in whispering copse and wood,
The distant voice of children's thoughtless glee,
   And maiden's song, are all one voice of good.

Amid the leaves' green mass a sunny play
   Of flash and shadow stirs like inward life;

The ship's white sail glides onward far away,
Unhaunted by a dream of storm or strife.

O Thou! the primal fount of life and peace,
    Who shedd'st thy breathing quiet all around,
In me command that pain and conflict cease,
    And turn to music every jarring sound.

How longs each gulf within the weary soul
    To taste the life of this benignant hour;
To be at one with thine untroubled Whole,
    And in itself to know thy hushing power!

Amid the joys of all, my grief revives,
    And shadows thrown from me thy sunshine mar;
With this serene to-day dark memory strives,
    And draws its legions of dismay from far.

Prepare, O Truth Supreme! through shame and pain
    A heart attuned to thy celestial calm;
Let not reflection's pangs be roused in vain,
    But heal the wounded breast with searching balm.

On a Beautiful Day.

So, firm in steadfast hope, in thought secure,
   In full accord to all thy world of joy,
May I be nerved to labors high and pure,
   And thou thy child to do thy work employ.

So might in many hearts be kindled then
   The lambent fire of faith,—not rashly strong,—
So might be taught to souls of doubtful men
   Thy tranquil bliss, thy love's divinest song.

In One, who walked on earth a man of woe,
   Was holier peace than e'en this hour inspires;
From him to me let inward quiet flow,
   And give the might my failing will requires.

So this great All around, so He, and Thou,
   The central source and awful bound of things,
May fill my heart with rest as deep as now
   To land, and sea, and air, thy presence brings!

SHORT-LIVED FLOWERS.

I MADE a posy while the day ran by:
Here will I smell my remnant out, and tie
    My life within this band;
But Time did beckon to the flowers, and they
By noon most cunningly did steal away,
    And withered in my hand.

My hand was next to them, and then my heart;
I took, without more thinking, in good part
    Time's gentle admonition,
Who did so sweetly death's sad taste convey,
Making my mind to smell my fatal day,
    Yet sug'ring the suspicion.

Farewell, dear flowers! sweetly your time ye spent,
Fit while ye lived for smell or ornament,
    And after death for cures:
I follow straight, without complaints or grief,
Since if my scent be good, I care not if
    It be as short as yours!

DEAD LEAVES.

YE dainty mosses, lichens gray,
   Pressed each to each in tender fold,
And peacefully thus, day by day,
   Returning to your mould;

Brown leaves, that with aerial grace
   Slip from your branch like birds a-wing,
Each leaving in the appointed place
   Its bud of future spring; —

If we, God's conscious creatures, knew
   But half your faith in our decay,
We should not tremble as we do
   When summoned clay to clay.

But with an equal patience sweet
   We should put off this mortal gear,
In whatsoe'er new form is meet
   Content to reappear; —

Knowing each germ of life He gives
    Must have in him its source and rise,
Being that of his being lives,
    May change, but never dies.

Ye dead leaves, dropping soft and slow,
    Ye mosses green and lichens fair,
Go to your graves, as I will go,
    For God is also there.

THE NIGHTLY SKIES.

When up to nightly skies we gaze,
Where stars pursue their endless ways,
We think we see from earth's low clod
The wide and shining home of God.

But could we rise to moon or sun,
Or path where planets duly run,
Still heaven would spread above us far,
And earth remote would seem a star.

'T is vain to dream those tracts of space,
With all their worlds, approach his face:
One glory fills each wheeling ball,
One love has shaped and moves them all.

This earth, with all its dust and tears,
Is his no less than yonder spheres;
And rain-drops weak, and grains of sand,
Are stamped by his immediate hand.

The rock, the wave, the little flower,
All fed by streams of living power
That spring from one Almighty will,
Whate'er his thought conceives, fulfil.

And is this all that man can claim?
Is this our longing's final aim?
To be like all things round, — no more
Than pebbles cast on Time's gray shore?

Can man, no more than beast, aspire
To know his being's awful Sire?
And, born and lost on Nature's breast,
No blessing seek but there to rest?

Not this our doom, thou God benign,
Whose rays on us unclouded shine:
Thy breath sustains yon fiery dome,
But man is most thy favored home.

We view those halls of painted air,
And own thy presence makes them fair;
But dearer still to thee, O Lord!
Is he whose thoughts to thine accord.

AT A SOLEMN MUSIC.

Blest pair of Sirens, pledges of Heaven's joy,
Sphere - born harmonious sisters, Voice and Verse,
Wed your divine sounds, and mixt power employ,
Dead things with inbreathed sense able to pierce;
And to our high-raised phantasy present
That undisturbèd song of pure concent,
Aye sung before the sapphire-colored throne
To Him that sits thereon, —
With saintly shout, and solemn jubilee,
Where the bright seraphim in burning row
Their loud uplifted angel-trumpets blow;
And the cherubic host in thousand quires
Touch their immortal harps of golden wires;
With those just spirits that wear victorious palms,
Hymns devout and holy psalms
Singing everlastingly;

That we on earth with undiscording voice
May rightly answer that melodious noise;
As once we did, till disproportioned sin
Jarred against nature's chime, and with harsh din
Broke the fair music that all creatures made
To their great Lord, whose love their motion swayed
In perfect diapason, whilst they stood
In first obedience, and their state of good.
Oh may we soon again renew that song,
And keep in tune with Heaven, till God ere long
To his celestial concert us unite,
To live with him, and sing in endless morn of light.

A THANKSGIVING.

Lord, for the erring thought
Not into evil wrought;
Lord, for the wicked will
Betrayed and baffled still;
For the heart from itself kept,
Our Thanksgiving accept.

For ignorant hopes that were
Broken to our blind prayer;
For pain, death, sorrow, sent
Unto our chastisement;
For all loss of seeming good,
Quicken our gratitude!

CHRISTMAS, EASTER, AND PENTECOST.

O du fröhliche, o du selige,
Gnadenbringende Weihnachtszeit!
    Welt ging verloren,
    Christ ist geboren:
Freue, freue dich, o Christenheit!

O du fröhliche, o du selige,
Gnadenbringende Osternzeit!
    Welt liegt in Banden,
    Christ ist erstanden:
Freue, freue dich, o Christenheit!

O du fröhliche, o du selige,
Gnadenbringende Pfingstenzeit!
    Christ, unser Meister,
    Heiligt die Geister:
Freue, freue dich, o Christenheit!

CHRISTMAS EVE.

THE sun is set, the stars begin
 Their stations in His watch on high,
As once around that Bethlehem inn;
 The vesper hour is nigh.

A little maid with eager gaze
 Comes hurrying to the house of prayer,
Shaping in heart a wild green maze
 Of woodland branches there.

One look, — a cloud comes o'er her dream;
 No burnished leaves, so fresh and clear,
No berries, with their ripe red gleam: —
 "There is no Christmas here."

What if that little maiden's Lord,
 The awful Child on Mary's knee,
Even now take up the accusing word: —
 "No Christmas here I see.

"Where are the fruits I yearly seek,
  As holy seasons pass away, —
Eyes turned from ill, lips pure and meek,
  A heart that strives to pray?

"Where are the glad and artless smiles,
  Like clustering hollies, seen afar
At eve along the o'ershaded aisles,
  With the first twilight star?"

Spare, gracious Saviour, me and mine:
  Our tardy vows in mercy hear,
While on our watch the cold skies shine
  Of the departing year.

Ere we again that glimmering view,
  Cleansed be our hearts and lowly laid;
The unfruitful plant do thou renew,
  And all beneath its shade.

By winter frosts and summer heats,
  By prunings sharp and waterings mild,
Keen airs of Lent, and Easter sweets,
  Tame thou the sour and wild.

And dare we ask for one year more?
  Yea, there is hope: One waits on high

To tell our contrite yearnings o'er,
    And each adoring sigh.

If He in Heaven repeat our vow,
    We copying here his pure, dread will, —
Oh, dream of joy! — the withered bough
    May blush with fruitage still.

NEW YEAR'S EVE.

Ring out, wild bells, to the wild sky,
   The flying cloud, the frosty light;
   The year is dying in the night;
Ring out, wild bells, and let him die.

Ring out the old, ring in the new;
   Ring, happy bells, across the snow:
   The year is going, let him go;
Ring out the false, ring in the true.

Ring out the grief that saps the mind,
   For those that here we see no more;
   Ring out the feud of rich and poor,
Ring in redress to all mankind.

Ring out a slowly dying cause,
   And ancient forms of party strife;
   Ring in the nobler modes of life,
With sweeter manners, purer laws.

Ring out false pride in place and blood,
  The civic slander and the spite ;
  Ring in the love of truth and right,
Ring in the common love of good.

Ring out old shapes of foul disease,
  Ring out the narrowing lust of gold ;
  Ring out the thousand wars of old,
Ring in the thousand years of peace.

Ring in the valiant man and free,
  The larger heart. the kindlier hand ;
  Ring out the darkness of the land,
Ring in the Christ that is to be.

IN THE WORLD YE SHALL HAVE TRIBULATION: BUT BE OF GOOD CHEER; I HAVE OVERCOME THE WORLD.

WHATSOEVER IS BORN OF GOD OVERCOMETH THE WORLD.

HE THAT OVERCOMETH SHALL INHERIT ALL THINGS, AND I WILL BE HIS GOD, AND HE SHALL BE MY SON.

WHOSOEVER SHALL DO THE WILL OF MY FATHER WHICH IS IN HEAVEN, THE SAME IS MY BROTHER, AND SISTER, AND MOTHER.

BELOVED, NOW ARE WE THE SONS OF GOD: AND IT DOTH NOT YET APPEAR WHAT WE SHALL BE, BUT WE KNOW THAT WHEN HE SHALL APPEAR WE SHALL BE LIKE HIM.

WHEREBY ARE GIVEN UNTO US EXCEEDING GREAT AND PRECIOUS PROMISES, THAT BY THESE YE MIGHT BE PARTAKERS OF THE DIVINE NATURE.

TRIBULATION WORKETH PATIENCE; AND PATIENCE EXPERIENCE; AND EXPERIENCE HOPE.

THE GOD OF HOPE FILL YOU WITH ALL JOY AND PEACE IN BELIEVING, THAT YE MAY ABOUND IN HOPE.

I COUNT ALL THINGS BUT LOSS IF BY ANY MEANS I MIGHT ATTAIN UNTO THE RESURRECTION OF THE DEAD.

GOD SHALL WIPE AWAY ALL TEARS FROM THEIR EYES; THERE SHALL BE NO MORE DEATH, NEITHER SORROW, NOR CRYING, NEITHER SHALL THERE BE ANY MORE PAIN.

WHEREFORE LET THEM THAT SUFFER ACCORDING TO THE WILL OF GOD COMMIT THE KEEPING OF THEIR SOULS TO HIM, IN WELL-DOING, AS UNTO A FAITHFUL CREATOR.

BLESSED BE GOD, EVEN THE FATHER OF OUR LORD JESUS CHRIST, THE FATHER OF MERCIES, AND THE GOD OF ALL COMFORT.

CONTENTS.

Asterisks signify that the Poems so marked are not given complete.

		PAGE
Evil．．．．．．．．．．．．．．．．．．．．．．．．．．．．．．．．	*Milnes*．．．．．．．．．．．．．	5
The Two Voices．．．．．．．．．．．．．．．	*A. Tennyson*．．．．．．．．．	7
Life shall live for evermore．．．．．．	*A. Tennyson*．．．．．．．．．	30
Evil shall end in Good．．．．．．．．．．	*A. Tennyson*．．．．．．．．．	32
*Oppositions of Science．．．．．．．．．．	*A. Tennyson*．．．．．．．．．	36
Through a Glass darkly．．．．．．．．．	*Clough*．．．．．．．．．．．．．	37
A World without God．．．．．．．．．．．	*Sterling*．．．．．．．．．．．．	40
*For Faith and Reverence．．．．．．．．	*A. Tennyson*．．．．．．．．．	43
*Christ in the World．．．．．．．．．．．．．	*Sterling*．．．．．．．．．．．．	45
*Plato and Christ．．．．．．．．．．．．．．．．．	*Sterling*．．．．．．．．．．．．	47
On a Life misspent in Vanity and Passion．．．．．．．．．．．．．．．．．．．．	*Petrarch*．．．．．．．．．．．．	49
Sin．．．．．．．．．．．．．．．．．．．．．．．．．．．．．．．．．．	*Herbert*．．．．．．．．．．．．．	50
For Forgiveness．．．．．．．．．．．．．．．．．．	*Donne*．．．．．．．．．．．．．．．	51
Enter not into Judgment, O Lord.	*Trench*．．．．．．．．．．．．．	52
*Discipline．．．．．．．．．．．．．．．．．．．．．．．．．	*Herbert*．．．．．．．．．．．．．	53
Dies Iræ, ．．．．．．．．．．．．．．．．．．．．．．．．	*Thomas de Celano*．．．．	54
Dies Iræ, translated by．．．．．．．．．．	*Trench*．．．．．．．．．．．．．	55
Under the Cross．．．．．．．．．．．．．．．．．	*W. C. R.*．．．．．．．．．．．．	60
Not This. From *Elegiac Poems*, through *Fosbery's Hymns and Poems*．．．．．．．．．．．．．．．．．．．．．．．．．．．．．．．		62
Christ's Cup．．．．．．．．．．．．．．．．．．．．．．	*S. Wilberforce*．．．．．．	64
Chastening ．．．．．．．．．．．．．．．．．．．．．．．	*S. Wilberforce*．．．．．．	65
Pilgrimage．．．．．．．．．．．．．．．．．．．．．．．．．	*Herbert*．．．．．．．．．．．．．	66
Pilgrimage．．．．．．．．．．．．．．．．．．．．．．．．．	*Trench*．．．．．．．．．．．．．	68

Contents.

	PAGE
The Way is Short............E. B. Browning.....	69
The Angel of Patience..........Whittier...........	70
Via Crucis Via Lucis. *Kosegarten*, translated by...........C. T. Brooks........	72
Πάθει Μάθος, (scattered stanzas from *A Vision of Poets*).....E. B. Browning.....	75
Adversa Mundi Tolera..........Thomas à Kempis....	76
Endure the World's rude Buffetings: the foregoing, translated by....................C. T. Brooks........	77
*A City that hath Foundations....Christina Rossetti....	80
"Rejoice Evermore "...........Trench..............	82
*To Sorrow.....................Milnes..............	85
Sad and Sweet................Aubrey de Vere......	87
*Love and Discipline.............Vaughan............	88
They are all gone...............Vaughan............	89
Vanished......................Wither.............	92
*De Profundis..................E. B. Browning.....	93
The Two Angels................Longfellow..........	96
Resignation....................Longfellow..........	99
The Alpine Sheep..............Maria Lowell........	102
Dear Friend, far off, my lost Desire.A Tennyson.........	105
The Past......................Bryant..............	107
Footsteps of Angels..............Longfellow..........	110
An Angel in the House.........Leigh Hunt.........	112
Be near me when my light is low.A. Tennyson.........	113
Do we indeed desire the dead....A. Tennyson.........	114
*In health, O Lord, and prosperous days. Anonymous. From *Fosbery's Hymns and Poems*................	115
The Sick Room. Anonymous. From *Fosbery's Hymns and Poems*...	116
Wholesome Memories of Pain. From *Elegiac Poems*, through *Fosbery's Hymns and Poems*..............	118
The Day of Death..............Trench.............	120
The Cloud on the Way.........Bryant.............	123

The Border-Lands. From *The Dove on the Cross*, through
Fosbery's Hymns and Poems 127
*The True Light. (From *The Sexton's Daughter*)............*Sterling*............ 130
Dust to Dust..... ....*Trench*............ 131
The Illusion of Life.............*Blanco White*....... 132
The Future Life................*Bryant*............. 133
The Return of Youth...........*Bryant*............. 135
Submission ....*Roscoe*............. 138
*Work.....................................*Whittier*............ 139
Work ....*E. B. Browning*.... 141
Employment..................*Herbert*............ 142
The same Dull Task and Weary
Way ....*Coventry Patmore*.... 144
*Imperfection of Human Sympathy ....*Keble*............... 146
Divine Order..................*Bonar*............. 148
Struggle not with thy Life.......*Frances Anne Kemble* 150
*Still Hope, Still Act......(From
The Sexton's Daughter).....*Sterling*............ 151
Hope for the Hopeless.........*Sterling*............ 153
Tu ne quæsieris................*Herbert*............ 156
Anticipation...................*Emily Brontë*........ 157
Onward into Light.............*Trench*............. 160
Carpe Diem....................*Trench*............. 161
Against Despondency. From *Elegiac Poems*, through
Fosbery's Hymns and Poems..................... 162
Against Foreboding............*Trench*............. 164
Vain Hopes and Fears.........*Trench*............. 165
They Serve who Stand and Wait..*Milton*............. 167
For God's sake. (The Elixir)....*Herbert*............ 168
Thou cam'st not to thy place by
accident ....*Trench*.... 170
*Adequacy......................*E. B. Browning*..... 171
My Times are in Thy Hand......*A. L. Waring*....... 172

Contents.

	PAGE
The Better Part. (To a Virtuous Young Lady)............Milton............	175
Fame. *Hymns of the Ages*, Second Series: there ascribed to *Schiller*............	176
*Truth........*Chaucer*, recast by *Milnes*..........	178
Duty...................*Wordsworth*.........	179
Peace...................*Alford*............	182
The Cloister...............*M. F. C*...........	183
The Worth of Hours............*Milnes*............	184
The Ingratitude of the Happy...*Trench*............	186
Were this World only made for Me...................*Princess Amelia*.....	187
Love's Self-Reproach............*Trench*............	188
Cast thy Bread on the Waters....*Barton*............	190
Example....................*Keble*..............	191
Absence...................*Frances Anne Kemble*	192
Disappointed Affection.........*Coventry Patmore*....	194
A Valediction................*E. B. Browning*.....	196
Friends parted by Opinion.......*Clough*.............	199
The Ministry of Love. *B. N.*, altered by................*Southey*............	201
The Kingdom of God..........*Trench*.............	203
My Psalm..................*Whittier*...........	205
*Andrew Rykman's Prayer.......*Whittier*...........	208
Veni, Sancte Spiritus. *Robert II., King of France*.....	216
King Robert's Hymn: the foregoing, translated by.........*F. H. Hedge*........	217
For Inspiration: Sonnet of......*Michael Angelo*.....	220
For Inspiration: the foregoing, translated by..............*Wordsworth*.........	221
For Inspiration...............*A. Tennyson*.........	222
*Self-Devotion and Resignation...*Keble*.............	223
*New Creation................*Whytehead*..........	225
For Grace..................*Herbert*............	228
*For Entire Devotion............*F. D. Huntington*....	230

Contents.

	PAGE
Watch, Pray, and Work.........*Frederika Bremer* ..	233
Ein' feste Burg ist unser Gott....*Martin Luther*......	234
A Mighty Fortress is our God: the foregoing, translated by.....*F. H. Hedge*........	235
*Morgenlied ....*Baron von Canitz*....	238
*Morning Hymn: the foregoing, translated in *Arnold's Sermons on Christian Life*.....................	239
Morgenlied ....*Klopstock*..........	244
Morning Hymn: the foregoing, translated by...............*Nind*...............	245
*Evening Hymn................*Keble*...............	248
Abide with me................*Lyte*...............	249
Emmaus.....................*M. F. C.*...........	251
Evening Hymn................*Sir Thomas Browne*..	252
*Sleep.......................*E. B. Browning*.....	254
*Praises for this World..........*E. B. Browning*.....	258
*Foregleams of a Heavenly Country. (From *The Monk and Bird*)...................*Trench*..............	259
*On a Beautiful Day............*Sterling*............	261
Short-Lived Flowers. (Life)....*Herbert.*	264
Dead Leaves. (Mortality)......*D. M. Muloch*.......	265
Nightly Skies.................*Sterling*............	267
At a Solemn Music............*Milton*..............	269
A Thanksgiving...............*Howells*.............	271
Christmas, Easter, and Pentecost.*Falk*................	272
*Christmas Eve................*Keble*................	273
*New Year's Eve..............*A. Tennyson*.........	276

www.ingramcontent.com/pod-product-compliance
Lightning Source LLC
Chambersburg PA
CBHW032104220426
43664CB00008B/1132